STUCK:

BETWEEN THE BADGE AND A HARD PLACE

Barry McKinley

ISBN 979-8-89428-929-8 (paperback)
ISBN 979-8-89428-930-4 (digital)

Christian Faith Publishing
832 Park Avenue
Meadville, PA 16335
www.christianfaithpublishing.com

Biblical references are from the Holy Bible, NIV.

Stuck: Between the Badge and a Hard Place, is a work of fiction. The names, characters, places, and incidents are products of the author's imagination or are used fictitiously and are not to be construed as real. Any resemblance to actual events, locales, organizations, or persons, living or dead, is entirely coincidental.

Cover design by Barry D. McKinley

Printed in the United States of America

CONTENTS

"There's only two good jobs—the one you're leaving and the one you're going to," or that's what my dad always said…in probably the most Southern accent you could imagine.

What I'd come find out later is that there's actually a third job—the one you're stuck in. I was stuck in this job because of what it's done to me. I didn't *think* like normal people anymore.

I'd basically traded my life for a life of *protecting* the public. You know, one of the good guys. Someone that could be trusted, respected, and looked up to.

A cop.

Little did I know was that this job can, and will, suck the life out of you. It will deprive you of peace, trust in others, trust in God, trust in yourself, and instead, replace it with an overall feeling of futility and hopelessness. Deep down I know that there's a plan out there and that I'm not the one in charge, but sometimes I can't see the big picture. These things that happen…they happen to everyone, for some reason, right? Maybe I'm just a little harder to teach than everyone else.

CHAPTER 1

Just Another Day at the Office

Someone always asks, "Were you scared?"
Short answer being, "You don't have time to 'be
scared' when you have the job to do. 'Scared' is a
weakness. 'Scared' is the possibility of cowardice
becoming a reality when you're the only thing
standing between crime and the victim. Sounds
like a God complex, but it's not. It's just the
reality that sometimes, people depend on cops
to protect them from the evils of society."

—Jimmy Mack

It's around ten thirty at night on a fantastically humid,
sweltering June night in a dimly lit alleyway cutting
through one of the rougher areas of town, and I was

1

chasing a bad guy that just robbed the corner market. The fine, upstanding citizenry watched on like they're watching a football game, yelling things and rooting for one of us. I just couldn't tell which one, but I had a pretty good hunch.

The city isn't much to brag about—not too big, not too small—and I'm certainly not gonna use the Goldilocks definition of "it's just right." It's far from that. I always thought that it was too big to have the small-town mentality and too small to have a big-city mentality. It just didn't *fit* its character. You know what I mean? It just wasn't *right*. It's kind of like the person who fakes everything—you know, where they're from, how they just "love" everything and everybody, and how "great" everything is. You know? Fake, just plain ole fake. The city smelled bad. It had a lot of empty storefronts, and a lot of major businesses started getting out of dodge. The unemployment was pretty high, and it had a government that didn't have the IQ above that of a gnat—or at least in my opinion. And no matter how hard they "tried" to bring vitality, it failed. The governing council members always seemed that they catered to either the rich or the poor extremes and pretended to get along, but in actuality, they hated each other's guts, just like a dysfunctional family. I don't really know how to describe it, but a lot of people said that there was "no quality of life here," which I totally agreed with. The crime rate for this place was *just* a tad high for the population, and by this time in my career, I'd become really jaded, cynical even. I'd been a cop for about ten years, and I'd seen a lot of pretty nasty stuff, been in a lot of nasty stuff, but to me tonight, it was just another day at the office.

"Beat 9 dispatch, suspect running south toward the cemetery!" I shouted into the radio, keeping a steady composure as I stayed just about ten feet behind the suspect I *personally* saw leaving the corner market with a gun and shooting inside the business. I'm running, I'm out of breath, I'm getting tired, and this guy won't stop.

"Copy that, Beat 9. 10-3, 10-3 for Beat 9. All units, 10-3 for Beat 9." Dispatch cleared the radio from all unnecessary radio chatter due to the emergency of the situation. An armed robbery is a pretty big deal, especially after shots have been fired at civilians.

Just in case you're not familiar with "cop talk" or police logistics, the city that I worked in divided the patrol areas into *beats*. Please don't ask me why they called them *beats*. It was just a geographic *zone* that was the patrol areas, and they were numerically increasing from *headquarters*, being the central zone, outward to the outer limits north, south, east, and west. It just so happened that Beat 9 was about a mile from headquarters to the south. There were a lot of *beats*. I think at that time there was somewhere in the neighborhood of sixteen or so *beats*.

"We're at the east gate of the cemetery at Riverside, heading into the cemetery!" I yelled into my radio.

"Beat 8's almost to him, Dispatch." Officer Covington let dispatch know that he's getting close to my position to help me catch this guy.

"10-4 Beat 9, Beat 8's en route." Dispatch acknowledged my position and relayed Covington's message in case I didn't hear it from Covington.

The adrenaline keeps you going, you know, not fear. It's part of that *primordial* fight-or-flight stuff they talk about. In all actuality, I didn't get worked up about this stuff anymore. It's old hat. Same ole stuff—go to work; get beat up or beat somebody up; get cussed out or cuss someone out; get suspended or get praised, get cut, stabbed, or shot; get called a white (*insert any bad name you'd like, or any derivation thereof*); stay late doing paperwork; go to court; go to the part-time job; go home long enough to take a shower, nap, change the uniform; and start it all over again. Oh yeah, if you're in a relationship, that takes a back seat even though your boss always says, "Take care of your wife" or "Take care of your kids" right before they tell you that you have to pull a double or sit guard on an injured suspect or God forbid watch over a victim who relives their hellish attack over and over while you sit by and try not to think about it because you've gone numb to the brutality of humanity.

Anyway, there I am. I'm gaining on this dude, and he's slowing down, and that's my cue.

Baby, I got him now! I thought to myself, and I push myself to run faster, lower my body to get that extra boost like a linebacker, and thrust my body forward to throw my shoulders into one of the prettiest takedown *spears* right out of a football game to force a fumble and into the guts of the bad guy just as he turned to see if was gaining on him. *Bam!* As his air escapes with a hollow thud and just as we're hitting the ground, he rolls over and sticks his gun right up against my head and…*boom!* The muzzle flash temporarily blinded me, and the sound of the gunshot set my ears ringing, but every sense in my body became supersensitive. I felt every grain of dirt grinding into my elbows and face. I tasted the blood in my mouth. I tasted the smell of the gunpowder—if that even makes sense. I felt like my whole head was in a furnace, and my left ear felt like it was…melting. I felt my heartbeat in every part of my body, but everything was in slow motion, and my vision was extraclear, like some sort of heightened *awareness*.

The bullet ripped right through my left cheek, but somehow, in this slow-motion dance with death, I was able to get to my service revolver (yeah, that's what we used to carry) and fire off three rounds. I saw him go down, and I tried my best to get up, but the ringing in my ears got superloud, and my vision was like one of those crazy movies with the camera zooming in and out, making me dizzy, and I felt sick to my stomach. My senses were crazy, and I didn't feel that I had any control of my faculties, but they were all intact. Well, my internal sensory checklist was kind of like *sight*: mostly check, *smell*: check, *taste*: yuck but check, *hearing*: kind of check, *feeling*: definitely check. I saw Covington running toward me, and I remembered reaching up and trying to tell him that the bad guy had a gun, but the world started spinning, and I got really nauseated and fell back down. All I heard was, "He's over here!" from someone who sounded like they were right next to me, and it scared me because I thought that an innocent may be hurt too, and then I heard Covington on the radio say, "Beat 8 headquarters, officer down, officer down! Suspect down. Get EMS in here!"

STUCK: BETWEEN THE BADGE AND
A HARD PLACE

Everything went dark, and I don't know anything else about what happened in that cemetery that night.

*****

I don't really know what happened out there, but when my eyes opened, I saw my friend Covington. I love him to death, and we've been through some stuff together, but he's not who I wanted to see when I woke up.

"Hey, Mack," he said in almost a whisper as he was leaning forward in the chair next to my hospital bed. He looks pretty rough, like he hasn't slept.

The best friend a guy could ever have was Todd Covington, or as so many of us called him, Covey. If I didn't know better, I would think he was in love with me, but that's just how loyal he was to our friendship. Big guy too. This dude's like 6'3", 260, and built like a truck and just as strong. Like I said, best friend a guy could ever have and really nice to have around when you need someone intimidated. Girls never shied away from him, and he seemed to have a certain charisma and charm that everyone loved. He really seemed to have his stuff together for a young guy, and honestly, I really admire him.

"We were kinda wondering how long you were gonna sleep, you lazy schmuck," he said with a half smirk under a nonuniform code, stubbly day-old beard.

I think I gave him a half-smile and said something that was supposed to be, "Why are you in my room?" because in my medicated mind, I was at home in my bed. He got that whimsical German shepherd look on his face and tilted his head to one side. You know the look that you get when you're trying to understand something in a movie, but the background music is too loud?

"What did you say? It sounded like blubbb-blubb…blablub," and he broke out in a really great belly laugh. I realized that maybe I should hold on to my questions for a little bit.

As my faculties began to recover, I remembered a bit of what happened just a few minutes ago, or so it seemed to me, and I knew I was in the hospital. But my head was absolutely killing me and making the thought process really painful. I didn't feel well at all.

"Where's Mary?" or that's what I thought I was saying.

"Dude, I'm sure that you think that you're making sense right now, but it's *not* happening," Covey said with a goofy I-can't-hear-you expression with the accompanying shrugging shoulders and pointing to his ears. All this gesturing to his ears and curious looking were making me just a tad on the angry side—pretty quickly too.

I can't really explain how quickly just being in a hospital can make you mad; or feeling like you're being mocked makes you mad; or the combination of pain, painkilling medicine, lack of mental and physical faculties, *and* being mocked…makes you mad. But I got mad really quick when Covey didn't answer me and kept that…that…that…*look* on his face.

"I want to know where my wife is, you refrigerator-looking gorilla!" I ranted with anger.

Covey and I have been best friends since his training days when I was his FTO, and I've known him for a long time *before* he was a cop. We've had ups and downs, but we've always had each other's backs and *generally* understood each other really well. He was like a gentle giant, and I was more like a no-nonsense, by-the-book kinda guy, but Covey didn't seem to really understand my anger at this point, and it was obvious that he didn't know what I was saying. He leaned back in the chair and had this really puzzled and hurt look on his face, and then he stood up and walked out. That was it; he just left.

What did I just do? I thought to myself as I dropped my head to that paper-thin pillow. This only served as a reminder that my head felt like it was literally being torn in half and only made my head hurt worse. My best friend in the whole world, the dude who probably saved my life—and I just treated him like garbage.

"Ungggh, eeeehhhhh!" was the best I could yell at the ceiling, but it wasn't any good because he'd already left the room and was probably halfway down the hall.

As I began to regain my faculties and started to acclimate to my surroundings, my senses began sharing the thankfully present beating of my heart, which now also took up residence behind my eyes, in my ears, and in my jaws. Did I mention that this one of the most horrendous headaches I've ever felt? I smelled gauze, iodine, alcohol, and that…that *hospital* smell. I tried to focus my eyes, and I could see the gauze around my eyes in the peripheral, and as I reached up, I felt gauze all over my face and my mouth, all while realizing—well, kind of—that my jaws were not opening when I tried to open them. Man, my face and head really hurt, and I just felt *sick*.

What seemed like an eternity ended when Covey came back in the room with a handheld mirror and a notebook. He looked at me with a look that I'd never seen before and said in a very soft and caring tone while he extended the mirror in his hand, "I wasn't joking when I said, 'I know you think you're making sense,' but, Jimmy, I can't understand a thing you're saying," and he held up the mirror. I took the mirror from his hand and moved it into position so that I could see my face and thought, *Yeah, I guess not*, with a sigh and a heavy heart. He gently tossed the steno pad on my chest and said with a light chuckle, "Maybe I can read your writing."

There it is. I didn't hurt my friend's feelings because there's no way for him to have understood me. The bandages covered the circumference of my head horizontally and vertically, and I looked like a really bad version of *the mummy*. While my mouth was not completely covered, there has a huge pad of bandages on the left side of my mouth, making it appear that I have the mumps. Apparently, they wired my jaw and did something underneath the bandages, but I'd have to wait and find out later. The old game show announcer came to my mind, *But wait, Bob, there's more*, as if I'd won all-expense-paid trip to Costa Rica or something. All I could do was snort a chuckle as I let the mirror fall to my chest, and Covey cracked a half smile.

"I guess that's gonna leave a mark," I mumbled, and I shrugged my shoulders, and I guess Covey created his own version of what I said and shrugged his shoulders, and with a sympathetic smirk, he sat down again and picked up the latest issue of whatever magazine was available from the lobby, and in this case, it was a women's magazine. I glanced over at Covey and grunted at him, pointing at the cover with a half shrug, and he looked at the cover and said with a grin and a chuckle, "Shut up, mumble boy." He won, so I just leaned back in the bed and stared at the ceiling and counted the heartbeats I felt in my head.

Covey browsed the pages for a few minutes then tossed the magazine on the table next to the chair.

"Ha, ha," he let out a laugh out of nowhere.

"I wish you'd been out there when Captain Davidson was en route to the scene," he said thoughtfully, as if he was remembering a great experience.

"Yeah, yeah. So EMTs were arriving, and I moved outta their way so they can work on you, and I called dispatch to let them know that the suspect was code 0, and Davidson snapped on the radio, 'You ain't no docta. How you *know* he's code 0, *Docta* Covington?'" while doing his best Captain Davidson imitation. Captain Davidson was one of those arrogant types who was condescending to everyone because he thought he *was* the world. You know the type of guy.

"So I, ha ha, say to him…" Covey started getting tickled telling me the story and started to chuckle a bit with a snort.

"Uh, Cap, I don't need to be a *docta* to tell that someone without a face ain't alive!"

And just as quick as he was laughing, he started crying.

"I thought I lost you, Jimmy," he said tearfully.

"You're family, and that out there"—he pointed to the outside world, outside of the hospital—"that scared me pretty bad, and…and you know I ain't scared of nothing but God," he said, trying to maintain his composure.

"I've never been this close to an officer-involved shooting."

I remembered that feeling the first time that I'd been involved in an officer-involved shooting. It was *not* pleasant, not to mention confusing. I mean, sure, they give you a badge and a gun and tell you to do the job. They train you on all the *laws* and the accepted *norms* for the use of deadly force, but they can't give you the internal acceptability or prepare you for the internal moral confusion. You know? The ability to live with yourself? The knowledge that you just took another human's life while doing your job? Sure, you tell yourself that it's part of the job and absolve yourself with, "It was him or me," but in the back of your mind, you always have a deep-seated guilt that gnaws at you a little less with the passage of time, but it's always there.

This was *not* what I signed up for. A lot of guys go their entire career without ever pulling their gun, except at the pistol range, and I'd been in two shootings in ten short years. And there it is—that *feeling*. That deep-down internal confusion. Listen, I know God's out there and that He's in charge, but He and I, we had a falling out a few years back. Don't get me wrong. I'm thankful that I'm alive, but I *feel* so dead inside.

Just then it hit me, and a surge of panic ran through me,

Oh no! What about the guy in the cemetery? I thought with a racing heartbeat and peppery feeling when the blood leaves your face.

I quickly grabbed the steno pad and started scribbling, and I showed Covey as he wiped his eyes and composed himself.

"What?" he asked in complete confusion,

"I told you the guy didn't have a face, Jimmy," he said, holding the notebook with open arms, as if to say, "What are you talking about." I quickly snatched it from him and wrote more.

He mouthed what I wrote and nodded his head.

"Oh, oh, yeah, yeah. *That* guy—the mystery voice," he said as he sat back down and leaned back into the chair and stared off into the distance.

"Yeah. I dunno, Jimmy. It was all kinda crazy out there, and I think I was just hearing things," he said, and then he got a shocked expression on his face and leaned forward, grabbing the arms of the chair.

"How do *you* know about that?" he questioned.

About that time, my pretty little wife came through the door, holding her mouth, and she seemed to be choking back tears. She slowly walked to the bed and touched Covey on the shoulder, and as he started to stand up, she said, "Stay there, Covey," she said as she sat on the side of the bed, patted my leg, and looked at me with those big doe eyes.

"I'm so happy you're okay," she said as she stroked my mummified face, and Covey looked in every direction to avoid that awkward fifth-wheel feeling. He stood up and hoisted his pants and announced, "So yeah," he said while he thumbed toward the door, "I'm gonna get outta here. I gotta meet IA in a bit, so, so I'll catch up a little later, okay?" He leaned forward and patted me on the forearm. "You call me if you need anything, Mary," he said as he backed out of the door.

CHAPTER 2

THE INVESTIGATION

No matter how much you try to *always* do
the right thing, there's *always* somebody there
to trying to trip you up, telling lies about
you…just to make themselves feel better.

—Todd Covington

"Let me tell you about Jimmy Mack because I know him. He and his kid brother are my best friends," Covey said as if he were orating a eulogy and getting worked up like a fire-and-brimstone preacher who needed breaths between each word. He hadn't even been asked anything difficult or offensive, but with Covey, it only took the word *inquiry* to get him twisted because of his past experience with Internal Affairs.

"No, Officer Covington, I need *you* to tell me the events of Friday, June 15, 1990."

Covey didn't really like Internal Affairs guys, and they knew it, and it came through pretty loud and clear in his tone of voice, his body language, and the *way* he said everything that came out of his mouth.

Covington began his statement.

"The call came out about Southside getting robbed. Suspect was a black male, about six two, 180 pounds with shots fired," Covington recapped while he leaned forward on the table in the interview room, with his hands open and karate chopping the table while explaining the events step-by-step. His elbows were glued to the table, and he stared deep into the eyes of Detective Grundy. Grundy tried to match Covington's stare and intimidation factor, but it wasn't working because Covington is a pretty intimidating man, especially when he starts talking in a low voice and deliberately succinct language. It's kind of scary.

"Mack called out on the radio that he was *literally* on top of the scene and saw the suspect run from the store and shoot into the store, then run south. He started calling out locations as he was chasing the guy on foot, headed toward the cemetery. I was about three blocks away and trying to get to him. As I turned into the east gate, I saw a muzzle flash then a couple more. I bailed outta my car and ran in the direction of the muzzle flashes, and I saw Jimmy on the ground. There's blood all over his face, and he's got his gun in his hand, and the suspect was on the ground about three feet away—"

"Hang on," Grundy interrupted. "How do you *know* it was the 'suspect'?" he asked in air quotes.

"What?" Covey got that look on his face that says it all—you know, the "are you stupid?" look.

"How do you *know* that was the suspect from the robbery?" Grundy is inferring that the suspect was a random citizen who was taking a leisurely stroll through the cemetery at ten thirty-seven at night.

Covey pushed himself back into the chair, keeping his body open and shrugging his shoulders in complete confusion, with his hands draped over the arms of the chair. He just looked at Grundy with a look that can best be described as a mix between disbelief and confusion. Covey's confusion lasted for a good minute as he glanced to the right and left with the same confused look on his face while he tried to rationalize the question.

"How do you *know* that was the suspect from the robbery?" Grundy demanded again, this time slamming fist on the table, raising his voice and squinting his eyes as he stared at Covey in the eye.

"I heard you the first time. I just can't figure out if I'm talking to the attorney for the ACLU or an Internal Affairs officer that's supposed to be determining the validity of an officer-involved shooting," Covey said with a rigid, cold stare into Grundy's eyes but with a calm voice.

"You'll answer the question Officer Covington!" Grundy yelled as he stood up from his chair.

Covey kept that curious look on his face as he moved his head to the left then to the right while he tried to figure out how to answer the question that, to him, seemed the dumbest question on earth, then he centered his stare back at Grundy, and his eyebrows raised in an *aha* moment.

"You're fishin'! You think this is a setup and that Jimmy's into something else!" Covey yelled as he stood up and pushed the chair back with the back of his knees and leaned forward pointing his finger in Grundy's face.

"You're wrong!" Covington yelled. "I've known Jimmy Mack for five years as a cop and a lot longer than that as his kid brother's best friend. He was my FTO. His kid calls me Uncle Covey." He continued yelling and pointing his finger in Grundy's direction.

"You got it wrong! And to answer your stupid question, I know it was the suspect from the robbery because Jimmy Mack said so!" Covey said with gritted teeth as he grabbed the back of the chair and slung it out of his way as he headed to the door.

"You're not finished," Grundy said as he stood up to face off with Covington, who towered several inches over Grundy.

Covington stared down into Grundy's eyes and said, "Yeah, yeah, I am. I complied with the interview regarding the officer-involved shooting on June 15, 1990, per standard operating procedure. Any questions beyond that event must be noticed to the officer being questioned at least ten days in advance, per SOP. Given that you have not given me notice of any further inquiry, we *are* done," Covington said as he stepped to his right to avoid touching Detective Grundy, and he stormed out of the room, slamming the door behind him.

I guess what most folks didn't know about Todd Covington was that he was intelligent, *really* intelligent. He had what I thought was an eidetic memory. The guy was the walking standard operations procedure manual and a legal library. But what he had going for him is that everyone *thought* that he was just a big dumb jock.

Grundy turned back into the interview room with a look of disgust on his face and threw his pen against the wall with gritted teeth and a muffled yell of anger "Ahhhhh!" He reached down and snatched the pen off of the floor and scooped up his notebook, tape recorder, and the IA file folder labeled "Mack: 88-IAB-291C"; adjusted his neck like he's trying to crack it, as he always does when he's agitated; took a deep breath; and closed his eyes as he snatched the door open.

Det. Dean Grundy was *not* what you'd call *normal*. Grundy was an army veteran who served in Vietnam and came home with a lot of baggage, just like a lot of guys did. So not knowing how to fit into society, he naturally found himself in the paramilitary profession of law enforcement. Even though the rules of engagement are entirely different, the rules, the order, the policies, the procedures—they all made sense to him and made him *comfortable*. His physicality made me think of a fireplug—you know, short, thick, and squatty.

He ended up in IA after he was involved in a shooting and had to be removed from active-uniform duty due to the injury that left him with a pretty noticeable limp. He refused to take the medical retirement because he was still young and viable. But the neck-adjusting thing when he's agitated—the jury's still out on just why he does that. Maybe it's just a tic.

Grundy, composing himself, gently turned off the light of the interview room and walked out and down the small corridor past the unit chief's open door as he heard, "Grundy!" He stopped after a couple of steps, dropped his head, and blew out his breath, as if to say, "Oh brother." He adjusted his neck, pivoted in a military about-face, and stopped in front of the door but didn't go in.

"How'd it go?" Unit Chief Dirkson asked.

"Great. Covington gave it up, told me everything," Grundy said with believability.

"Really?" Dirkson asked with sarcasm and an eyebrow raise.

"No, not really," Grundy said in a muffled yell as he entered Dirkson's office, as deflated as a cheap pool float after its first use, but then he composed himself as he realized who he was talking to.

"What are you doing, Dean?" Dirkson asked.

Grundy, obviously frustrated and feeling defeated, paced in a confused small circle and then a figure eight before throwing himself into a chair like a rag doll and said, "I don't know, Terry," as he blew out his breath in defeat.

"I've been after this guy for the better part of two years. I've got a photo. I've got a snitch. But I can't corroborate either one. The photo was taken by a ghost, apparently, and…and the snitch…ha ha, boy there's a winner for ya." Grundy continued with hand gestures and ended with a *pffft* and throwing of his hands in the air.

"I think I'm going to help you out here," Dirkson said as he gazed at Grundy across his desk with his head leaning to one side and with a small nod and letting his bottom teeth envelope his top lip.

"Yeah? You gonna get me a witness? You…you gonna give a confession?" Grundy was obviously getting worked up as he stood up from the chair, dropping the file and the recorder from his lap. While he's reaching down to snatch up his dropped tools of the trade, he continued his frustrated tirade. "You gonna show me the money? You gonna show me the connections? What? What are you going to do to help me out, Terry, huh?" Grundy ended his tirade with his signature neck adjustment.

"It's over," Dirkson said in a calm and commanding voice.

Grundy stopped dead in his tracks. "Over?" he asked in disbelief. "What-what do you mean over?"

Grundy was completely dejected as he felt his insides turn and twist.

"Over, file closed. Off. Jimmy Mack's officer-involved shooting of June 15, 1990, is a justified shooting, and he is cleared—period. No offshoots unless you have evidence. You remember evidence, right? The stuff that we use to *prove* that someone committed a crime. The stuff that we present to grand juries and petit juries to secure a conviction of a crime wherein someone is proven guilty *beyond* a reasonable doubt," Dirkson said in an increasingly terse tone, as if explaining to a cadet the finer principles of case preparation, investigation, and presentation and obviously getting worked up enough to drink half a bottle of Pepto.

"But," Grundy injected with disbelief.

"There is no *but*, Dean," Dirkson said while standing up from his chair but still behind his desk and beginning to raise his voice higher,

"There is no *anything* to the…the…the allegation that has caused you to become obsessed with Jimmy Mack for the past two years. This is my fault for not having your head examined and letting you go down this rabbit hole, goose chase," Dirkson continued in a fueled single-breath tirade.

"Allowing you to entertain the idea that just because a photo of unknown origin pops up," Dirkson reiterated.

"And allowing you to entertain the story of a convicted drug dealer accusing a cop of being a drug kingpin was wrong on *my* part, but I'm stopping it here and now. Unless you have something solid, you *will not*—and let me be clear—you will *not* investigate any allegations against Jimmy Mack unless you have *evidence*! Am I clear?" Dirkson said with increasing frustration, emotive body language, and head shakes.

Standing in disbelief, Grundy adjusted his neck. "Crystal," he said as he pivoted in an about-face to leave Dirkson's office.

CHAPTER 3

WHO NEEDS FEELINGS?

Feelings are an unnecessary emotion when it comes to this job. *Feelings* are too expensive and too extravagant. They weigh you down and keep you in this quagmire of confusion that threatens to envelope your entire being, drowning you each and every day over and over. But as a human, you have to have *feelings* if you ever want to have relationships with other living creatures. My problem was that I thought that I could control whether or not I had feelings, but I found out that they were issued to me as standard equipment, part of the whole Jimmy Mack experience.

—Jimmy Mack

It was so real. I could see everything. I could hear everything. I could feel every emotion.

"Ahhhhh!" I screamed as I woke up in that hospital bed with those ever-present hospital smells wafting through the air—the bed whose mattress was little more than three inches thick and so uncomfortable that my bones felt as if they were filled with concrete, the bed that was making my joints painful to the touch and my butt numb. Twisting and turning, just trying to get comfortable, but *nooooo*, that's not possible because the bed is so narrow and short and thin. You can't really adjust to it because there's an IV coming out of your arm, these stupid wires to that stupid machine, the stupid side rails. You get that it's frustrating, right?

I was shaking and sweating, and my heart was pounding in my temples. I felt like crying. I felt mad. Everything was this tangled mess, just like Christmas lights in a bundle that you'd *thought* you had coiled so perfectly last year, only to realize that certain things intrinsically lend themselves to always being a tangled mess-like *feelings*.

I'm goin' nuts, I thought as I cupped my eyes to shield them from the fluorescent light that seemed to shine directly into my brain, intensifying the thumping in my head.

I thought about my wife and felt like crying. I felt like there was a hole where my heart is or where it was. Where was she? Why wasn't she here? Did something happen to her? I know I just saw her, or did I? It feels that I've been here forever.

I thought about my daughter, and I got happy then sad, an emotional roller coaster. See why I don't like *feelings*? Up and down, mind racing, questions, crazy answers—it's all so much internal drama. Christmas lights.

What's my baby girl gonna think? How's she gonna react to...to whatever's under this roll of gauze? I thought to myself, getting more and more worked up as I kept talking to myself.

This is making my head hurt. All this...this *feelings* garbage. I don't like 'em. Not necessary equipment. I just need to keep my head together. Forget the other *stuff*. Logical and steady—yeah, that's it.

What's got you worked up, Jimmy? I questioned myself as if I were interrogating myself as a suspect in some heinous atrocity, but I was a suspect—suspected of being weak and not being able to be strong enough to handle whatever life threw at me without falling apart. How many other things can possibly go wrong in my wretched existence? The first shooting, then the *accident*, now this shooting. The accident bothered me more than anything. That really changed everything.

Knock it off, Jimmy! I yelled in my head.

Then just as quickly, my thoughts changed to think that I needed to talk to my wife about this, but what is *this*?

Great! I thought to myself, or maybe I even groaned out loud.

What time is it? I wonder as I looked around for a clock. No clock. Awesome.

I looked around for the TV remote, not really thinking *that* would be an easy find. I had to flail around all over the place, getting madder and madder because I couldn't find it. Yep, there it is, clipped to the sheets at the top of bed for "my convenience."

I just spent twenty minutes looking for this stupid thing, I thought as I felt my blood boil with anger.

"Ahhh!" I yelled out in frustration. Man, I'm angry!

What are you mad at, dude? I asked myself.

I know myself well enough to know that they must've given me morphine because it affects me in some of the most negative ways. This internal blabbering and headaches are just to name a few.

My head is killing me. My butt is numb. My joints hurt, and I haven't seen my wife or daughter, and I can't talk. What's there *not* to mad about? I thought as I attempted to throw the TV remote across the room in frustration, only to have it gently pull from my hand and fall next to head of the bed.

Yeah, that was cathartic, I thought in total sarcasm, and I let my head fall to the paper-thin pillow, blowing out my breath. Seems like I would've learned to not let my head fall, but the fall allowed me the subtle realization that my head was feeling like I'd been run over by a truck and, judging from the throbbing, a pretty big truck.

That's a stupid thing to say, Jimmy. A truck is a truck, I logically deduced, as if I were Sherlock Holmes, and I tried to inject my attempt at self-humor,

Actually, my dear Watson, any vehicle striking the human body would suffice in making one feel that way, I said to myself in a probably pretty terrible, snobbish English accent.

Little did I know that standing at my room door was my pretty little wife, watching me with tears in her eyes. I had no idea how long she'd been there. My head was hurting so bad that I thought if I pushed my palms into my eye sockets, I could get some relief. Yeah, no joy there. As I took my hands from my eyes, I saw her, and she slowly walked to my bed and sat down on the side of the bed.

STUCK: BETWEEN THE BADGE AND
A HARD PLACE

It was obvious that she didn't know where to put her hands on my face as her eyes welled up with more tears. After all, where could she put them? My whole head was, well, encased in a gauze helmet. She decided on a great, big, warm hug, and then she pushed back, saying, "I talked to the doctor. But before I do that, I wanted to explain why I haven't been here."

"It's okay, sweetie. You're here now." Or that's what I was trying to say, but you know how it came out, right? Yeah, you guessed it: "Gung gung-gung," etc.

"Jimmy, I-I-I can't bring Hannah here," Mary said, stuttering and shaking her head side to side and starting to get emotional.

"Not yet. She can't see you like this. She won't understand. She won't." Mary said as she gently collapsed onto my chest, sobbing.

Oh God, this is killing me, I thought as I held her close to try to take her pain.

Stroking her long black hair usually did the trick, but it wasn't paying off this time. She sat back up so that she could look at me in the face with tears in her eyes, and then she got the look that let me know that she was getting mad but then quickly calmed herself and exhaled.

"So the doctor says that you're the luckiest man alive," she said as she fiddled with the collar of my hospital gown.

I already know that, I thought to myself as looked at her.

"This bullet, the one that has you looking like 'the mummy,' she said with an emerging smile and a giggle, "it did an amazing feat. Sure, it went down the side of your face, but when it hit the joint of your jaw, it glanced off, and it didn't even break a tooth," she said as she announced the miracle.

"They wired your jaw shut just for a little while to let the muscles, tendons, and junk like that heal. But your ear, well, we'll see about that later," she continued, pleased with her explanation, now finished fiddling with the hospital gown. She seemed happy, content even. But just that quickly, I saw it in her eyes. She was getting angry again.

"What were you thinking, running after that… that, scumbag?" she said with increasing irritability, and then all of a sudden, she slapped me on my shoulder and then collapsed into my chest, sobbing.

See what feelings get you? I thought.

She's going through the same garbage that I'm going through, the roller coaster, and you know the difference? She's allowed to have feelings, but for me, it's a weakness.

STUCK: BETWEEN THE BADGE AND
A HARD PLACE

I have to be strong and keep it all inside. I'm a cop, and I can't afford feelings on or off the job. You remember that, right? I explained to myself.

But hey, that's great that the damage is minimal, right? I changed the subject in my mind.

My Mary is a superstrong woman. She can handle anything. She kept me together through the accident, through my first shooting, and the birth of Hannah, and she should probably wear a cape.

She's about five feet two inches, just around 105, and just melts me like an ice-cream cone on the Fourth of July. Long silky black hair, beautiful big brown eyes, and so very beautiful inside and out. Athletic, smart, funny—the total package. And most of all, she's crazy about *this* guy. They say you can't love someone if you don't love yourself, but I hate myself for what I've put her though. That's the *feeling* that I have for myself, and it's really hard to reconcile those feelings of self-loathing with the feelings of such deep love for Mary and Hannah. They contradict each other. *Feelings* are confusing, just like tangled-up Christmas lights.

CHAPTER 4

DENNY

There are a lot of strange, unexplainable things
that happen. If not to us, then to someone
we know, and we may never put the pieces
together, but if you dig long enough, you'll
find a common denominator—God."

—Rev. Dennis Mack

Right outside of the hospital door of Jimmy Mack
was his younger brother by seven years, Dennis Mack,
but everyone called him Denny. He was sitting in a
chair and positioned to see anyone who came into
the hall and ready to escape in a minute's notice. He
was leaning forward with his elbows on his knees and
rocking back and forth, praying.

STUCK: BETWEEN THE BADGE AND
A HARD PLACE

Jimmy and Denny were close growing up, but the accident changed all of that. Jimmy and Mary kept Denny after the accident up until Denny made his career choice of the ministry. Jimmy almost disowned Denny for that decision, but each man maintained his position, and Jimmy chose to not keep in touch with Denny. Denny, on the other hand, kept a watchful eye on his wayward brother.

Mary walked down the hall toward Jimmy's room, distracted by putting her keys into her purse, but as she looked up and saw Denny, she dropped her purse and ran to him and threw her arms around his neck. In total shock and relief, she pulled away from him, and then she hugged him again, "I'm so glad you're here."

"I've been here every day, Mary, just when no one can see me, and I guess I didn't expect you yet," Denny said sheepishly, and he looked around to make sure that there weren't any witnesses to his visitation.

"Why?" Mary asked with a look of hurt in her eyes and tilting her head to one side as she examined Denny's face.

Denny is a great preacher, a great speaker, but not so good when it came to talking about his brother or his *feelings*. There seemed to be a common familial pattern between the two men, so divided in their convictions yet so similar in so many respects. The accident did a real number on both of the men. Denny pulled *closer* to God, and Jimmy pushed *away* from God.

"C'mon, Mary. You know why," Denny said with an air of "I don't want to talk about this again,"

"I don't need anyone telling him that I was here, him getting upset, and, you know," Denny said, like a child trying to explain the F on his report card.

"Don't be silly. I'm sure that he wants to see you, Denny," Mary said while she gently rubbed his arm in a consoling manner.

Denny kept his head down and turned around to leave. Mary could see that he was visibly uncomfortable as he looked back at Mary.

"I don't know, Mary," he said as he stayed confused about whether to stay or leave.

Like any good distraction at just the right time, Covey walked down the hall toward Jimmy's room. Covey's face lit up like a kid at Christmas when he saw Denny, and he opened his arms and walked toward Denny. Covey grabbed Denny and hugged him like a long-lost brother.

Covey and Denny go back further than Covey and Jimmy. Covey and Denny went to school together, so even though Jimmy *knew* Covey growing up, they weren't close until Covey joined the police department. But Covey and Denny—they were really close friends. Covey and Denny played football together in high school, and most of all, Covey was there for Denny after the accident that took Denny's leg and his parents, but somehow, Denny found "the peace that surpassed all understanding." Don't misunderstand. Jimmy was there for Denny after the accident but had his own issues to deal with at that time. So Covey was a godsend for Denny, and along with Rev. John Dowdy, Denny would decide his path.

"Man, I haven't seen you in forever," Covey said as he pushed Denny back to arm's length to look at him like he was inspecting something for damage, but he kept Denny's arms held between those huge hands.

"Yeah, yeah, I know," Denny said, looking down, and then to one arm that was grasped by the huge vise grip, and then to the other, using his eyes to express the fact that Covey hadn't let him go yet.

"Oh, yeah, yeah." Covey quickly released him.

"So how's it, eh, how's it going?" Covey asked as he tussled his hands into his pockets, shrugging his shoulders, kind of uncomfortable now.

Denny got that look on his face that said it all. Every emotion that he was not willing to admit that he had was right there on his face. He took a deep breath and said, "Yeah, it's great. Um, you know, the church is getting along, getting a little bigger. Um, yeah. And you, what about you, huh?"

Covey looked at Denny, with a tilted head and a saddening expression on his face.

"I…I'm good, Denny. But you know," Covey said with an opening of his palms that he let fall to his side, but he stopped himself from saying anything more and quickly changed the subject.

"Have you, um, have you been in? Yeah, he looks great. Right, Mary?" Covey said as he looked toward Mary with an approving nod and then back at Denny.

"Yeah, great," Mary said with a fake smile, trying to reassure Denny that Covey was telling the truth.

"C'mon, guys. I see that you're really uncomfortable here. I know he looks like a mummy. I've seen him. I haven't let him see *me*, but I've seen him. I also know that he's a walking miracle because of the dance the bullet took. Being a minister has privileges," Denny said with conviction and, in a way, to let Mary and Covey know that he knew what was going on.

"Let's get some coffee, huh?" Covey asked in an attempt to redirect the conversation and lead Denny away from the room so Jimmy might not hear the conversation that was escalating in tone.

"Mary?" Covey asked Mary, as if a *yes* would be like the prettiest girl agreeing to go to the prom, and Mary nodded in agreement with a forced smile, raised eyebrows, and crossed arms, obviously very uncomfortable.

"I really shouldn't have come," Denny said as he ran his tongue in his closed mouth across the front of his teeth in an effort to keep from saying anything else that he was thinking. He turned to start walking away.

Covey saw that Denny was not on board with staying or getting coffee, so his hands dropped to his thighs in defeat. As Denny was walking away, Covey touched his shoulder to get him to turn around, "C'mon, Denny. It's been such a long time, and you guys are brothers," Covey said in a gentle voice, and then he started motioning with his hand, pointing between Jimmy's room and Denny. "This…this isn't good, and it hurts seeing it, and I *know* it hurts being in it."

"Listen, Denny. You may be the younger one, but you're probably more mature," Covey said, trying to rationalize with Denny.

"I'm…I'm sorry. I shouldn't have let anyone see me. That's what's been working for a couple of days, and I should've paid more attention to the time," Denny said, as if he'd made the biggest mistake of his life as his eyes filled with tears.

As Denny turned to leave, Covey lunged forward, as if he was grabbing a suspect to keep them from running, and he pulled Denny into a bear hug, cupping the back of Denny's head and throwing it into his chest. Denny broke into an uncontrollable sob. Another victim of *feelings*.

Mary looked on, feeling the pain that Denny was experiencing, and she silently sobbed as she cupped her mouth. *Feelings*—the pain of people you love hurting so badly.

The statuesque Covey had tears slowly rolling down his cheeks as he embraced the sobbing Denny—yet another victim of *feelings*.

Was Jimmy Mack, right? Were feelings unnecessary? The everyday struggle of the never-ending roller coaster of feelings, up and down, side to side, tossing its riders like a rag doll. Does untangling the Christmas lights year after year really help? Do feelings serve a greater purpose? Do they connect people or disconnect them—or both? Do they connect a person *to* God or disconnect a person *from* God—or both?

CHAPTER 5

MARY AND HANNAH

It's hard being married to a policeman, fireman,
EMT, soldier, or even an electrical lineman…
never knowing if they're coming home. The
only piece of mind you can have is to take
it for granted that they are coming home…
to keep the fear from eating you up inside.

—Mary Mack

"What's wrong, Mommy?" Hannah asked Mary as
she slowly opened Mary and Jimmy's bedroom door
at home.

Mary was crying, and little Hannah wanted to
know why. In Hannah's little mind, Mommy crying plus Daddy not being home equals something's
wrong. Mary hadn't told Hannah about her daddy

41

yet because Mary didn't know *how* to tell her, so she did what every good mother would have done—told a little white lie. Mary told Hannah, "Daddy had to take a prisoner to another state all of a sudden, but he'll be home *real* soon, baby." And that's what Hannah believed, at least at first, but now she saw Mommy crying again.

"Is Daddy hurt, Mommy?" Hannah asked with eyes as big as the moon, slowly filling with tears half as big as her eyes.

Hannah is a beautiful, intelligent, and kind four-year-old who is well advanced for her age. Mary would always say that Hannah is *gifted* but never really explained her assessment of what *gifted* is. Everyone knew that Hannah was a gift from God for the young couple and an angel in her own right, and she was born at just the right time in the couple's life. Some of the most intellectual people in the community were always fascinated with how smart Hannah is, and the conversations that she was able to understand and take part in made everyone think that the child was a genius.

"You can tell me, Mommy," Hannah said in a reassuring tone as she patted Mary's shoulder with her little hand.

Mary burst into a full sob as she grabbed Hannah and held her tightly, cupping her little head.

"I'm sorry I didn't tell you, baby girl," Mary cried apologetically.

Hannah pushed back to look at her mother's face, both with tears in their eyes. Hannah squinted the tears from her eyes and got a composed look on her face as she pushed Mary's hair out of her face and examined Mary's face with her eyes. "I know Daddy's okay, Mommy. God told me," Hannah said with complete reassurance.

Jimmy had stopped going to church after the accident, but Mary found reassurance there. She knew that Jimmy was a very strong man, but she also knew that he was having a serious issue with God. She would *only* pray about it, but she'd never broach the subject with Jimmy. In her mind, *it was complicated*. But then again, what relationship isn't?

Mary, on the other hand, did not stop going to church, staying active, and taking little Hannah. She maintained her faith and instilled that same faith and passion in Hannah. She and Hannah prayed with devotion for Jimmy that he would "be protected from the evil one and restored," which was the prayer that Hannah made up. Quite a big prayer for such a young child.

Mary stopped sobbing immediately, and her mouth fell agape as she just stared in disbelief at

Hannah. Hannah just smiled at Mary and said, "I knew that you were trying to keep something from me, so I prayed."

Mary, still in disbelief, gently cupped Hannah's face and said, "Oh, my baby. What...what do you mean that you *knew* that I was keeping something from you?"

Hannah, still wearing that soft, gentle smile, said, "You haven't been yourself, Mommy, and it started when you said that Daddy had to go out of town. I knew you weren't telling me the truth, so I decided to ask the One who knows everything—God."

Mary had a very apparent chill run down her spine as she shuttered, and the entire moment had an eeriness to it.

"And...and...and what exactly did, um, God tell you, um, baby?" Mary asked as she pushed the hair away from Hannah's face, all while wiping the tears from her own eyes and sniffling to ready herself for this conversation.

Hannah stopped smiling and looked at Mary and said, "He didn't actually *say* anything, but I knew Daddy was hurt and that I should pray. I just felt that everything was okay, so don't cry, Mommy." Hannah said all of this with such a matter-of-fact confidence that Mary could only feel comforted by this four-year-old.

Mary, not even realizing it, had loosened her grip on Hannah, which made Hannah's pushing back from Mary easy, and Hannah just turned and walked out of the room as if there were no more concerns.

Mary must've realized that she was dumbfounded and shook her head in disbelief. She wiped the drying tears from her face, wiped her hands on the front of her jeans, and stood up. She sniffled and, as if trying to appear composed, pulled the bottom of her shirt to adjust it, and she walked to the door but stopped. There was a smell in the room that she couldn't quite place. It was sweet. It was soothing—kind of weird, in fact—but just that quickly, it was gone. Then she shook her head again to rejoin reality.

Is that even possible? she thought to herself. *Did I just make that up in my mind to make myself feel better for lying to my daughter?*

"Hannah!" Mary called for Hannah as she walked down the hall to Hannah's room.

She walked into Hannah's room to find the little one putting on her raincoat.

"What are you doing, baby?" she asked.

Hannah was still looking down at the task at hand—the buttoning of the raincoat. "I'm getting ready, Mommy."

"Ready for what, sweetie?"

Hannah stopped and looked at her mother with a look of aggravation on her face and said crossly, "I'm getting ready to go see my daddy."

Mary just looked at Hannah and said, "Hmm. Oooookay," and in bewilderment, she could only think to do what Hannah wanted.

Who'd have thought? A four-year-old. Humph, Mary thought to herself as she went to retrieve her own raincoat.

The two fought the drizzling rain to get into the hospital and meandered through the mazes of hallways and elevators to get to the hallway leading to Jimmy's room. The unmistakable hospital smells and sounds only increased the anxiety that the two were already feeling as their walk seemed endless. Mary was holding Hannah's hand, and she said, "Now, Daddy might be asleep, but you can see him, okay?"

Hannah looked up with her big blue eyes and was starting to get frightened, and Mary saw it. The two stopped, and Mary knelt down and gently held Hannah's little arms.

"If you don't want to go, baby, we can leave," Mary said in that soothing, motherly tone.

Hannah struggled with internal dialogue for a few seconds and looked at her Mommy and said, "Nope. I'm good," and she stepped back away from her mother and started walking down the hall, as if she knew where she was going, causing Mary to stand up and catch up with her.

They stopped just outside of Jimmy's room, and Mary looked in to see him sleeping.

"He's asleep, sweetie," Mary whispered.

"Can I hug him?" Hannah asked softly.

Mary picked Hannah up, and they walked softly to the side of the bed, and Mary leaned down so Hannah could touch her daddy. She touched the bandages and examined him with her eyes with such love and compassion, and a single tear fell from her eye as she turned away to hug Mary, silently crying. Mary quickly ushered Hannah out of the room so as to not wake Jimmy and to comfort her.

"It's okay, baby," Mary said as she tried to stay composed to appear strong for Hannah. The two stopped and sat in the hallway lobby, with Hannah on Mary's lap.

"Listen, Hannah," Mary said as she pushed the hair away from Hannah's face.

"Daddy's fine. The bandages are just covering his face until it heals, but the doctors say he's going to be just fine," she explained as she smiled at Hannah.

"He *probably* won't be able to hear out of his left ear, which might not be *too* bad," she said comically, tickling Hannah, causing Hannah to giggle just a bit and smile.

Mary adjusted Hannah's raincoat and stroked her face. "I think we should go home and eat some dinner. What do you think?"

Hannah agreed with a nod and a smile.

CHAPTER 6

THE CHASE FOR JUSTICE

The only thing necessary for the triumph of
evil is that good men should do nothing.

—Edmund Burke (circa 1920)

The city is not too far adrift from that of the likes of
Chicago, Atlanta, Detroit, Philadelphia, Portland, or
the hundreds of cities across this fair land exceeding
populations of a million. However, it doesn't have
that large of a population. It was what classifiers
might call *midsize* (population of one hundred thousand to five hundred thousand).

But like other places to live—city or town;
small, mid, large—there were *good* places, and there
were *bad* places to live. Of course, no one wanted

49

to live in the *bad* places, but some had no choice. Others who didn't want to live in the bad places had to make a choice too: work hard at more than one job, get a really good job, or move. And like every other place on this planet, there are good and bad people in both good and bad places to live.

No one *knew* Anthony Albritton. No one knew where he was from. No one knew who his parents or grandparents were. No one remembered him from school. But strangely enough, he was elected mayor six years ago. Imagine that. Nothing verifiable and yet elected mayor at the first toss of the hat.

Calvin Jackson, though, was another story. *Everyone* on the south side of town and the police department knew Calvin, his brother, his parents, his grandparents, and anyone who claimed to be related to him. Calvin was what one would call *bad news*.

Peculiar duo, in fact, Albritton and Jackson—one with absolutely *no* history and the other with *nothing but* history. How and why did these two pair up? You see, Albritton was the owner of Southside Corner Market, the store that was robbed and left Jimmy Mack with certain *distinguishable* scars. Jackson was the "manager" of Southside Corner Market and was also an integral part of Jimmy Mack's past, a past that fueled a deep-seated loathing that ate at Jimmy Mack's very soul, a loathing that Mack himself would admit was unhealthy and not logical but was burning his very soul and made him stand at the gates of hell every day.

Five years before the shooting

About seven months after Anthony Albritton was elected mayor, he appointed Calvin Jackson to be head of the recreation department without any consideration of qualifications—or rather lack thereof—and with no input from the council members. It was shocking to much of the police department and certainly the citizens of the south side of town because Calvin was no stranger to criminal activity. The problem was that there were no *felony* convictions to go with his label of *gangbanger*. The folks in town had questions like, "Who makes a dope boy the head of recreation?" Statements like, "I thought he said he was gonna get *rid* of the 'gang problem' here, but he's puttin' 'em in charge," were commonplace, but nothing changed the charismatic hold that Albritton had over the community. And almost as if meeting the Lord, Calvin Jackson seemed to have turned over a new leaf and became a respectable member of society…with the help of Albritton, of course. This reeked of "good ole boy politics," but in this size of city? Confusing for sure, but remember that the city is too big to be small and too small to be big. Albritton was within his authority to appoint Jackson, according to the charter, because there was a vacancy.

Albritton also introduced new community strategies to curb crime and *empower* the citizens, making sure to acknowledge their efforts at regular town hall meetings. It was not uncommon for Albritton to engage the neighborhood-watch members throughout the city by acknowledging them with awards and citations for "exemplary service to the community" and making them *feel* important in their own *zone*, which was a geographic designation created by Albritton. It was almost as if Albritton was allowing the citizens to *self-govern* to an extent.

Many police officers were suspicious of this miraculous decrease in crime. Some even thought that Albritton was paying the criminals to keep them less active. This was *not* what the chief of police wanted to hear his officers talking about or even speculating that the mayor was in fact a criminal himself. The chief even suspended a few officers for being overheard entertaining that possibility in public while they were on dinner break. Jimmy Mack was never suspended for speaking the censored words, but he surely thought it.

Jimmy would oftentimes work the late and midnight shifts on the south side of town for some reason. It seemed that the watch commander always stuck him down there. Maybe it was because he'd developed a few sources that panned out and made the stats look good, or he was aggressive on patrol, but whatever the reason, you could almost be sure to find Jimmy on the south side.

There's that miserable schmuck, Jimmy thought as he saw Ray leaving the club on Madison. Ray Wilson was a drug user who could only be described as a loser who would never amount to anything because *he* was his own worst enemy.

Jimmy stayed in his squad car with the headlights off, cruising the street like a shark on patrol as he followed Ray a good length back. Jimmy could tell that Ray was high by the way he was walking—or more like strutting—like a drunk chicken. Just before Ray walked through the open lot at the corner of Madison and Hanover, Jimmy made his move and skidded to a stop in front of Ray and jumped out of the car. Jimmy had Ray by the collar and slung up against the car before you could say, well, anything.

"What's up, Ray," Jimmy said as he was patting Ray down and holding him against the car. You see, Ray was on probation, so he was always fair game for inquiring law enforcement because of the stipulations of his release.

"Whoa, whoa, whoa there, Jimmy," Ray said while he tried to appear calm, cool, and composed, and he held his hands up. "I'm just…I'm just…you know what I'm sayin'. I'm just chillin', headin' home." Ray tried again to appear dignified and innocent as he adjusted his collar.

"Yeah? What time is it, Ray?" Jimmy asked with a sarcastic tone.

"I don't know. About what, nine?"

"Are we in Samoa, Ray?" Jimmy asked sarcastically.

"Wrong answer there, Ray!" Jimmy said while raising his voice. "It's 4:00 a.m., but I'm pretty sure that you knew that now, didn't you?" Jimmy stepped back, spun Ray around, and looked him in the eye with obvious frustration, as if *he* was Ray's probation officer.

"Now, what time are you supposed to have that pretty little head on the pillow for your beauty sleep there, princess?"

Ray just hung his head because he knew he was caught.

"C'mon, Jimmy, dude. It's hard. You know what I'm sayin'?"

"Well, that's gonna cost you, ain't it, Ray?" Jimmy said, as if he just won the lottery.

Ray exhaled and just looked up to the sky, and said, "What you lookin' for, Jimmy?"

"I don't know, Ray. What've you got that's gonna keep you from gettin' violated?" Jimmy asked as he spun Ray back around against the car, handcuffed him, and put him in the back of the squad car.

Jimmy wasn't arresting Ray. It was the *show* so that the onlookers wouldn't think that Ray was "snitchin' to five-O." Sort of a cover, if you will. Did it work? Who knows, but it's the best that a cop can do.

Jimmy took off with Ray in the back seat and slid the cage window open.

"I'm listening, Ray," Jimmy belted as he drove away from the lot.

"If I give you *this,* you gonna have to leave me alone *forever,* bro," Ray said, as if he was going to testify against Al Capone.

"We'll see, Ray," Jimmy said, thinking that there was no quality of information that would flow from Ray's mouth.

Ray obviously was having a conversation with himself based on the pregnant pause between Jimmy's last statement and the beginning of Ray's information.

"All right, look. Calvin Jackson's running junk out of Southside," Ray announced with a nod.

It's a good thing that there was not a lot of traffic on the road because Jimmy weaved over into the other lane as he looked in the rearview mirror at Ray.

"What? Does Albritton know?" Jimmy asked inquisitively.

"I don't know what Albritton knows. I know that Calvin has Rico trippin' to Miami twice a month. They cook it up, and it flows outta Southside. The dollars flow right into Calvin's bank account. He even has a couple of them schoolboys sellin' for him," Ray said with full conviction and certainty of his information.

Jimmy could feel himself getting angry. He knows Calvin's type, flashing a couple of bucks in front of kids who never get anything because of poverty, making himself seem like a millionaire. And those are the kids who get the short end of the stick.

For what? A couple of bucks and ghetto notoriety until they go to prison?

Jimmy pulled into an empty warehouse parking lot and unpacked his cargo.

"So what? That's it?" Ray asked, as if he was going to receive the key to the city.

"Yeah, Ray, that's it. No parade. No balloons. No speeches," Jimmy replied, all while he's unlocking the cuffs from Ray's wrists.

"But you know what, Ray?" Jimmy said in a I'm-in-a-generous-mood tone with accompanying hand gestures. Jimmy reached into his wallet and pulled out a twenty-dollar bill and handed it to Ray.

"You're your own worst enemy, Ray. You're a smart man, but you're killin' yourself. I'm not gonna preach at you, but what I *am* going to do is pray for you. I hope you use that to get something to eat, not to smoke or shoot up. And I truly hope and pray that one day, we'll see each other, and you'll be a different man."

CHAPTER 7

THE ORIGIN OF ANGST

I never knew that doing the right
thing would cost me so much.

—Jimmy Mack

Armed with newly acquired information from Ray, Jimmy Mack cruised the alley behind Southside Corner Market. This was *not* the easiest place to surveil because of the windows, the streetlights, and the overwhelming amount of people who seemed to never go home. Nonetheless, Jimmy was on a mission. He knew that Calvin Jackson was up to something, and he just found out that it was crack cocaine! Did Mayor Albritton know? Probably, but there's no proof...yet.

"Think about this a minute, Jimmy," he said to himself.

"How would Ray know this?" he asked himself.

"Ray *is* a crackhead. He *would* know where to score and who was selling, right?" he justified to himself.

Just as he was pondering the veracity of Ray's statements, he saw Calvin come out of the back of the corner market, holding a small grocery bag, and get into the passenger's side of a brand-new black 1985 Lincoln Town Car. The same black Lincoln Town Car that belongs to Joseph "JoJo" Townsend, a convicted cocaine dealer who just got out from doing a five-year stint for possession with intent. It seemed strange to go from prison to a brand-new Lincoln, but *maybe* JoJo invested wisely from "the yard."

Yeah right.

"Well, well, well. Ray wasn't lying *this* time," he chuckled to himself.

Hmm, I wonder what sort of business they have at 5:00 a.m. It is a market, so the bag doesn't mean any-thing because he could just be "tending to his customers," right? Jimmy thought to himself as he jotted his notes. Date, time, activities—regular surveillance stuff.

I wonder what sort of business got JoJo that new Lincoln? he chuckled again with a sarcastic thought.

The Lincoln sat with JoJo and Jackson in it, with the motor running for a good five minutes before Jackson got out…empty-handed, of course. JoJo slowly drove down the alley, and Jimmy made sure to make notes of how long Jackson and JoJo were together. Jimmy let the Lincoln get a little bit farther down the alley and made sure that Jackson was inside the store before he started to follow JoJo.

"Huh, look at that," Jimmy said to himself with a false befuddlement. "That *brand-new* Lincoln has a defective taillight. I think I'll let JoJo know that his brand-new car has a defective taillight, and it's an absolute outrage that they just don't make 'em like they used to," Jimmy said out loud and with a smirk on his face, knowing that he just got himself some probable cause to at least stop JoJo.

*****

On the other side of town, Jimmy's younger brother Denny and their parents were getting ready to take Denny to the high school to get on the bus for an away game. Not a *big* game or anything, just the state championship.

The Mack family was pretty close-knit. They all got along, and even the boys, Jimmy and Denny, were close despite the seven-year difference in their ages. The family wasn't rich, wasn't poor, but was able to be comfortable with what Jimmy's father made at the paper plant and his military retirement.

Jimmy and Denny's parents, Glen and Ada, were really *good* people. They'd been married for over thirty-five years and got along really well, loved each other a lot, loved their kids, and really loved God. They were supportive of their children's endeavors and raised them to be respectful, hard-working, and God-loving young men.

Denny was in his senior year in high school and struggling with his future, but he decided for right now that he was just going to *enjoy* his senior year. He was a really bright and athletic teenager, but he had issues deciding what he wanted to do with his life. He'd thought about college, the military, technical school, or even following Jimmy's path in law enforcement, but he just couldn't decide. He never found that *passion* that everyone talks about, that *calling*, as it were. He was good at whatever he did once he learned it, but he never had a *preference* for anything, not even football. He was the proverbial "worker bee," a *follower*.

"Excited?" Ada asked as she was getting Denny's travel cooler ready with all the snacks he could possibly want.

"Nah, not really. I'm just going to, well, *go*. It's not like I've got a scholarship or anything, so when it's over here, it's over," Denny said with a kind of nonchalant air, almost defeated before the game even started.

"I *know* that doesn't mean that you're going to play *halfway*, right, son?" Glen spoke as he peered over the top of his glasses with that look that says, "Don't make me come over there."

"No, sir, not anything like that. It's just got me bummed out a bit—you know, one more game, then graduation, then *life*," Denny orated as if he was giving eulogy for his life up to that point, and he exhaled a long sigh.

Glen and Ada both smirked and looked at each other, nodding their heads with an offset eye roll, as if to say, "Oh, brother."

Denny realized how corny that sounded, so he looked back and forth like a really bad stand-up comedian with a goofy look on his face and said, "Wha-whadda you want outta me, huh?" causing the equally cornball laugh.

"No, seriously, guys," Denny said, trying to be serious. "After this game, after graduation in the spring, I got nothin'." He seemed truly perplexed.

"You don't have *any* pulling in *any* direction, son?" Glen asked as he leaned forward on the table, folding the newspaper and setting it down. By this time, Ada had come over to stand next to Glen, with both parents listening intently to their son's dilemma.

Glen didn't really know what to think about Denny's lack of direction, so most of the time, he just stayed silent. Glen had learned a lot about life because of his military career, which started before Vietnam but ended shortly after Vietnam, and it seemed that Vietnam left a bitter taste to his mouth. Even though he was proud of his service, he never spoke about his time in Vietnam. In a way, Glen wanted Denny to go into the service because of the direction and discipline that it would offer but always worried that some *conflict* could throw his son into the same grinder that he ended up in, so silence was his best advice on the military. He just wanted his sons to be happy and productive Christian men.

Ada also always wanted the best for her boys, and she would remain silent as long as they were doing "what they loved." "Just do what you love," Ada would sing like a songbird, but for Denny, that didn't work because he didn't know "*what* he loved" to do.

"Pop, it's like, well," Denny said as he searched for words with meaning.

"Not being able to describe something that you're lookin' at," he finished, and he sat back in his chair, obviously feeling frustrated because he couldn't articulate what he wanted to say.

Glen and Ada glanced at each other with a concerned look, and then Glen stared Denny in the eyes and asked, "Have you prayed about it, son?."

"Pffft!" Denny let out his air in frustration.

"Don't get me wrong, Dad. Either He's not talkin', or I'm not hearin'," Denny explained.

Ada sensed the young man's frustration building, and knowing he needed to keep his head ready for the game, she turned around and started fiddling with the dish towel while she was putting it in its place and said, "Well, before next spring, you'll have your answer, I'm sure. But for now, we've got to go get you to that bus."

"And you need to drive because I forgot to get gas last night." Ada added, "So there. That's 'your calling' for today," causing a little courteous chuckle from Glen and Denny.

*****

Jimmy waited for the Lincoln to clear the intersection before he turned on the emergency lights to stop JoJo. Well, it was Jimmy's *intent* to stop JoJo, but JoJo had other plans and hit the gas.

"Beat 8 to dispatch. In pursuit, black Lincoln Town Car. Xray-Delta-Hotel-469 west in the 700 block of Highland Ave. Driver JoJo Townsend," Jimmy belted into the radio, clear and calm, just like Jimmy always was.

JoJo was headed to the west side of town, most likely hoping to get to the bypass to head out of town. Maybe he'd be able to get the Lincoln up to top speed, but only if he can get there.

"Beat 5 dispatch, headed east on Highland in the 1200 block, getting ready to cross Garrison Avenue," Officer Conley alerted dispatch and Jimmy that he was closing in and ready to divert the fleeing Lincoln.

Garrison Boulevard was one of the main arteries through town, always with a lot of traffic. Jimmy and Conley both knew that they couldn't have the Lincoln careening through Garrison's red lights and possibly killing anyone. JoJo was already hitting sixty-five miles per hour on Highland, which is a residential area, and the chase was leaving a bad feeling in Jimmy's stomach.

Conley did a power slide and blocked the intersection just short of intersection of Garrison and Highland, which was just ahead of JoJo, forcing JoJo to turn left into yet another residential.

"He's not gonna make it to Garrison, Beat 8. He's on Cherry," Conley announced over the radio.

Now the problem comes in making sure that JoJo doesn't make it to Inner Perimeter Road, where he can still loop around the city to hit the bypass. But the other south and west side units were all on calls, and Conley was now *behind* the chase, leaving the city wide open for JoJo. Neither the county sheriff's office nor the state patrol was close enough to do any good at JoJo's rate of speed, and this was starting to look like a disaster in the making.

"Beat 8 dispatch, he just hit Inner Perimeter, northbound," Jimmy advised as he started getting a little nervous. He'd been in a lot of chases, but this one was starting to get a little dicey. It'd only take JoJo about five minutes to make it to the bypass at the eighty-five miles per hour that he was now doing, plus running the traffic lights that seemed nonexistent to the careless driver.

"SPV 6 to Beat 8," Sergeant Dillon called for Jimmy.

"Go ahead, Sarge," Jimmy responded.

"I need you to fall back, Jimmy. Let him go. We know who it is. Issue the warrant, and we'll pick him up later," Sergeant Dillon ordered calmly and succinctly.

STUCK: BETWEEN THE BADGE AND
A HARD PLACE

"Copy, SPV 6. Terminating at Inner Perimeter and McIntosh," Jimmy announced to dispatch to document the end of the chase.

Jimmy turned off his emergency lights and started falling back further. JoJo was already pretty far out in front, and Jimmy didn't know if JoJo saw that he was giving up, but he surely was hoping that he did.

*****

A little less than a mile from the terminal point of the chase, Denny, Glen, and Ada were in Denny's little Chevrolet Chevette, Jimmy's hand-me-down car, heading east on Westtown and going through the big dual four-lane intersection of Inner Perimeter and Westtown, when the black Lincoln driven by JoJo careened through the intersection against a red light at around eighty miles per hour, striking the passenger side of the Chevette and tearing the car in two, ejecting the young driver and vomiting him out almost into the parking lot of the corner convenience store. As the Lincoln tore through the remnants of the Chevette, it swerved diagonally left across the intersection and hit a light pole head-on, throwing JoJo through the windshield, with his lifeless body

67

being launched over the hood of the Lincoln another fifty feet into the parking lot of a restaurant that was just opening, with early morning customers watching the carnage in horror.

CHAPTER 8

THE ORIGIN OF ANGST 2

I can't believe that I saw *what* I saw. I can't
believe that my whole life would change
in an instant, and I caused it all.

—Jimmy Mack

Even though Jimmy wasn't chasing JoJo anymore,
he was still close enough to see the carnage of the
accident before returning to his beat. Jimmy watched
helplessly as the accident unfolded right before his
eyes. He saw the sparks from the impact and the huge
billowing dust cloud mixed with emissions, and he
felt his stomach turn like never before in his life. He
watched as the thousands of pounds of metal inter-
mingled with each other and spewed fluids from the

mechanisms, and parts were tossed around like feathers in the air from the violence of the impact. He watched as the massive land yacht devoured the small compact car like it was a snack for the Jolly Green Giant.

The police department's chase policy was actually quite restrictive, and Jimmy was pretty much violating that policy when he gave chase to JoJo. He had the probable cause—the defective taillight—but the speeds were highly questionable, and the distance at which he could follow was questionable. Nonetheless, he initiated the chase, and even though he turned off his emergency lights to let JoJo know that he wasn't pursuing him anymore. The freshness of the termination would bring about repercussions for sure. But Jimmy thought for sure that he could articulate a potential drug exchange to bring about the felony-chase clause. But that's being a cop—decisions and dealing with consequences of actions.

As Jimmy came to a halt in his squad car, Sergeant Dillon pulled up to block the traffic from the west. A feeling of sickness fell over Jimmy as the nerves in his head began to tingle, and he felt like he was going to pass out. He'd never experienced this, and despite all of the stuff he'd been through in his short four-year career, this was bad because his action had *major* consequences.

Jimmy recognized the car that the Lincoln had decimated. The feeling of dread intensified. Nobody had a Chevette anymore, or at least it looked like what was left of a Chevette. He knew it was Denny's just because of where it was and when it was, plus *he* used to own it. He remembered the black rally stripes that he put on the rocker panels that made the positive identification as certain as a morgue identification.

"Oh, my Lord, no!" Jimmy yelled as he ran toward the remnants of the Chevette.

Sergeant Dillon recognized the little car too and ran to grab Jimmy and tackled him in the intersection. By this time, in what seemed like hours but was actually only minutes, several other officers had arrived, EMTs were arriving, the fire department was closing in, and there were people from the houses whose backyards joined Inner Perimeter Road and Westtown Road gathering around in their bathrobes. The convenience store patrons and the drivers of the now-stopped traffic looked on in horror at the catastrophe, wondering what had happened. The smell of the biscuits being cooked at the restaurant mixed with the smell of gasoline and vehicle fluids being carried by the fall breeze created a very unappetizing aroma. The smoky backdrop of steam from radiators and burning fluids on hot exhaust created an eerie haze against the backdrop of blue-and-red emergency strobe lights and mercury streetlights.

Jimmy let out such a soul-emptying scream that no mere mortal could describe. This was truly the *utterance* referred to in the Bible when the Gospels speak of the Holy Spirit making intercession on our behalf. Dillon fought to hold Jimmy back. Both men struggled one with the other, one protecting the other from carnage and the other trying to get to his family in hopes that he didn't just witness their demise.

"What did I do?" Jimmy screamed as he fought to get away from Dillon.

The young driver Denny was ejected approximately forty-seven feet from the vehicle as it literally *opened* up upon impact and spit him out. He was pretty badly beaten up and would most likely lose his right leg, but he was alive.

The same could not be said for Glen and Ada. Both were killed on impact, and for the sake of all that's holy, the injuries will not be described, only to say the car was torn in half as the Lincoln drove through it.

JoJo was also killed, not so much by impact with the Chevette but by being catapulted through the windshield. Later, it would be learned that the brown bag that Jimmy witnessed being handed to JoJo contained $5,000 in cash, and there were two kilograms of cocaine found in the trunk of the Lincoln.

"I-I-I just need to…," Jimmy sobbed while he grabbed Dillon's shirt.

"I can't let you go up there, Jimmy," Dillon said with a heartfelt denial while holding Jimmy.

"I did this, Sarge." Jimmy's tears were streaming down his face as he looked at the carnage, in the smoky haze with the flashes of emergency lights and the pungent odors of oils combining with the crispness of freshly fallen leaves and biscuits. It was a cornucopia of sensory confusion.

"You couldn't have known, Jimmy," Dillon rationalized.

"But I didn't *have* to chase him," Jimmy tried to explain, which only made his sorrow more and more deep.

"You can't do this, Jimmy," Dillon said as he was trying to make Jimmy realize that there were more moving parts in the universe than just his actions.

Officer Grayson came running up to Dillon and Jimmy, who were still on the ground, and announced,

"They're taking Denny to Grace General. He's rough, but he's alive."

Jimmy looked at Dillon in disbelief, who was still holding him. Jimmy started tussling with Dillon with renewed vigor.

"You gotta let me go. Let me go!" Jimmy yelled as he seemed like a man on a mission and recharged to fight with Sergeant Dillon, who himself was a pretty big guy.

Dillon reinforced his grip on Jimmy and looked him in the face and said sternly, "I'll take you, but you are *not* driving anywhere! Got it?"

Jimmy nodded in defeat as they both got up off of the pavement. Dillon kept a pretty good grip on Jimmy as they walked way around the wreckage to Dillon's car, with Jimmy trying to get a look into the remnants of Denny's car. He didn't *know* if his parents were in the car until he saw sheets inside the car covering bodies. He knew that Denny had an away championship game, and their parents always—I mean *always*—sent him off with their full support. Dillon put Jimmy in the passenger side and ran around to the driver's side, and they drove away in full emergency mode.

"SPV 6 to dispatch," Dillon spoke into the microphone very calmly and in charge.

"Go ahead, SPV 6," dispatch called back.

"En route Grace General. Have an oncoming two-man unit go the 10-50F and pick up Mack's car and take it to PD."

"10-4, SPV 6."

Dillon never once showed any emotion. USMC through and through even in civilian life.

"Thanks, Sarge," Jimmy said in a calm, steady voice as he stared blankly through the passenger window.

Dillon never said a word. He knew there were so many moving parts to this. Department liability, Jimmy's liability, Jimmy's parents, Jimmy's kid brother, Jimmy's pregnant wife, and Jimmy.

Dillon and Jimmy arrived at the emergency room entrance at the same time as the EMTs carrying Denny. Before Dillon stopped the car, Jimmy launched himself out of the car and toward the ambulance that was coming to a stop in the first bay of the platform. As the doors to the ambulance opened, Jimmy tried to get into the back with Denny, but the EMT, Jerry Nance, pushed him back. "Jimmy, Jimmy, we gotta get him inside."

"I know. I know, but I need to see that he's okay," Jimmy pleaded.

"He's not, and he's not going to be if you don't let us get him inside, Jimmy."

Jimmy had been on the job long enough to get to know firefighters, EMTs, nurses, doctors, and so many other first responders. It would be nice to say that this knowledge made his situation easier, but it didn't. Jerry knew that Denny needed attention, and that was much more important than trying to give preferential treatment to his fellow first responder.

The ambulance driver had made it to the back of the unit by then and joined the restraint of Jimmy. Jerry had been partially successful in keeping Jimmy away from Denny and the gurney, tussling the whole while, but now the EMT who was driving was involved, and the tussling stopped. The driver, a new EMT named Robert Dawson, and a really large fellow grabbed Jimmy by the collar with one hand and moved him to one side so that Jerry could release the gurney to roll it in.

"I'm here, Denny!" Jimmy yelled to Denny while being restrained by Robert and Jerry wheeling the gurney in at top speed. That's about the time that Dillon got there, grabbing Jimmy and pushing him to the side so the EMTs could do their job.

Jimmy stopped squirming and pushed back from Dillon in a seriously aggressive form and scowled while looking at Dillon, as if there was going to be a seriously nasty fight. Jimmy started taking deep breaths, as if preparing to deadlift five hundred pounds, and he lowered his head but raised his eyes to look at Dillon and, in a soft but stern voice, said, "I did this to him. I killed our parents. I am responsible for him. I am his brother. Do *not* put your hands on me again. Got it, Sarge?" and pushed Dillon away.

Dillon, a former combat marine and veteran police officer who had seen his share of domestic combat as well, knew that Jimmy was getting mad, but he stood his ground and then grabbed Jimmy.

"Now you listen to me, boy. I know you've got a lot going on right now, but you don't want to end up laying there next to your brother, do ya?" Dillon said, matching both calmness and sternness.

CHAPTER 9

THE DEFLATED SOUL

How do you comfort a man that feels
responsible for destroying his family?

—Mary Mack

A solid knock on Mack's door accompanied by a
two-burst ring on the doorbell awakened Mary from
her sleep. In a daze and barely conscious, she opened
the door to see a uniformed police officer standing
there, and her heart sank, and her knees gave way,
and she collapsed into a small pile into the entryway.
Everything that could go wrong was now right in
her face. Every spouse of every officer in the world's
nightmare was in her doorway. "No, no, no!" she
cried in disbelief and denial.

STUCK: BETWEEN THE BADGE AND
A HARD PLACE

Even though Mary had been through this before when Jimmy was shot, there was no *conditioning* or amount of preparedness that a spouse can have. There is no "getting used to it" when it comes to having these uniformed visitors. As the sun began to rise, filling the entryway with yellow hues and the light breeze bringing the smell of fall, the pregnant Mary rocked back and forth in disbelief as this memory was being etched into her memory.

"Mrs. Mack?" the young officer asked as he knelt down and touched her shoulder. He had no idea who Mary was. He didn't know Jimmy. The department was small but not so small that everyone knew everyone.

"I need to take you to the hospital, ma'am. Your…your husband is there and needs you. Seems there was an accident involving his parents, and he's in no condition to drive," the polite young man said in a pastorally soothing tone as he reached down to offer her a hand.

With a confusing sense of relief, Mary was able to stop crying and realize that Jimmy wasn't killed but that he *needed* her. That was the catalyst that she needed, but why was she relieved? She knew that something happened to his parents. How could she be so selfish? On one hand, she was glad that he was okay, and on the other, she was mortified that something happened to her in-laws. But what if this young officer was not telling her the truth, and Jimmy really *was* dead, and he just wasn't supposed to be the one to tell her? What if she was dreaming, and this was all just a freakishly real nightmare? *All* this internal dialogue happened in an instant, the proverbial blink of an eye.

Mary, six months pregnant, tried getting up from the floor and reached up to grab for help from Officer Day, who quickly braced her forearm to help her to her feet as she was wiping the tears from her eyes. "Please come in and give me just a minute. Please." Mary allowed Officer Day to enter the house.

"Can I get you anything, ma'am?" Officer Day asked in an effort to minister to her needs.

Mary just nodded as she walked toward the back of the house. Officer Day had been on the job for a total of three months and was just off training, and this wasn't a task that he was quite up to. Chasing bad guys, writing traffic tickets—those are what he signed up for, not condolence calls, not trying to comfort someone related to him only by the "thin blue line."

Mary waddled back into the hallway, adjusting her coat around her pregnant belly, and grabbed her keys and purse. She stopped and took a deep breath, closed her eyes, and exhaled.

"Okay, let's roll," she said, as if she were a police officer herself and trying to inject levity into the situation.

She pulled the door shut and shook the doorknob and made her way to the passenger's side of the squad car with Officer Day opening the door for her.

"I'm sorry, ma'am. It's a little tight," he offered his apologies for the lack of legroom.

Mary looked at him and, trying to make light of a bad situation, said, "And what exactly are you saying, Officer?" with a smirk on her face.

Officer Day wasn't sure that she was playing and appeared mortified but then saw her grin.

"Yeah…um, right," he said as he shut the door and reemerged on the driver's side.

As they headed toward the hospital, Mary sat, quietly rubbing her belly, and tears gently flowed down her cheek as she asked, "What happened?"

"I don't really know, ma'am. I just got on duty. I was told to come and get you because your husband needs you at Grace General."

"Grace General?" Mary inquired with a puzzled look on her face. "Was Jimmy on the west side of town?"

"I don't know that either, ma'am," Day answered while keeping his gaze on the road ahead.

Mary just quieted down and sat there as they continued toward the hospital. Day just did what he was told to do—drive. As they got closer to the hospital, Mary's fears, hormones, and anxiety got the better of her, and she started sobbing as Day pulled into the roundabout driveway at the emergency room. Mary sat in the car sobbing, but she suddenly composed herself and got out of the car and walked to the door of the emergency room. As the doors opened, the smell of alcohol preps and that *hospital* smell hit her in the face, and her fears overcame her, and she ran into the emergency room, franticly looking for and yelling for her husband Jimmy with tears in her eyes. She had been told only enough to make her sick to her stomach, and her imagination did the rest.

As Mary ran by the nurses' desk, the rather heavyset nurse who favored a professional linebacker jumped out of a chair and grabbed Mary. "Hold on, baby! Where do you think you're going?" the nurse asked in a stern but caring way.

"My…my husband's here. His family's… he's here. He's a policeman," Mary stammered and stuttered.

"Okay, sweetie, you mean you're here for Jimmy and his brother. I need *you* to calm down 'cause it don't look like you're far enough along to give birth, and the way you're upset, it ain't gonna do you or that little angel any good. Now come with me, and let me get you some water and let you sit down. I'll go get him."

You know that feeling when everything is surreal? Your face has that numbness, your lips are dry, and you feel like you're going to pass out. That was where Mary was emotionally and physically. The two worlds met, and suddenly, all she could do was vomit. The dizziness caused by the lack of blood flow and the adrenaline mixed with the emotional roller coaster of not knowing were just more than she could stand.

"Oh my goodness, baby," the nurse said as she came into the room and handed the cup of water to Mary. She quickly turned around to grab some hand towels that were under the cabinet to clean up the mess.

As the nurse struggled to get up from the crouching position, she looked up at Mary and said, "I've known Jimmy for a long time, sweetie. All I can do is pray for the both of you and tell you that I'm so very sorry."

Mary sat there with all sorts of bad thoughts and questions racing through her mind.

She's so sorry, Mary thought. *What in the world happened?*

Jimmy turned the corner into the room with Mary with tears filling his eyes. "I killed them, Mary," he said, and he fell to his knees and let his head fall into her lap. Mary had an indescribable look of horror on her face as she cupped Jimmy's head, rubbing it to soothe his pain.

"What…what do you mean, baby? Killed who?" Mary asked hesitantly.

Jimmy let out another soul-retching groan that shook Mary's heart with pain. She could *feel* the deep-down ache that her husband felt, as if their souls were connected in agony. She knew that it was bad. Her husband was one of the strongest men she'd ever known, and for him to be this distraught meant that it was *bad.*

Jimmy lifted his head to look at Mary and started his story. "I was chasing JoJo, and he ran the light. He hit their car. My god, Mary. I couldn't…I didn't know. Mom and Dad are gone, and Denny's in the OR. I've never seen anything like it. Oh, my Lord Jesus, what have I done?" And then he let his face fall into her lap, sobbing.

Mary didn't quite get the full picture, but she understood enough to know that Jimmy was in a bad way. He just lost his parents, and his brother was hanging on by a thread, plus it all happened while *he* was doing *his* job, the job he where he thought he would make a difference…for the better, the job that he'd always wanted as a child—the good guy.

Mary held his head closer in an attempt to get him as close to a hug as she could and gently kissed the top of his head while she stroked his hair. "Oh my poor baby," she whispered. Mary just kept staring past Jimmy's head onto the floor with tears gently and silently rolling down her cheeks, not knowing what to say, what to do, or how to do it. Mary just kept rocking Jimmy's head in her lap, and she looked to heaven. "Dear Lord, we need You," she whispered.

CHAPTER 10

THE REALIZATION

Be strong, and let us fight bravely for our
people and the cities of our God. The Lord
will do what is good in His sight.

—Rev. John Dowdy,
referencing 2 Samuel 10:12

Back to the present

As I lay in my hospital bed, all I could do was *think*.
Think about this; *think* about that. Think, think,
think.

Do you know what happens when you think
too much? You have regrets.

Do you know what happens when you have
regrets? You have emotions.

Do you know what emotions are? *Feelings*, stupid feelings. Did I ever tell you how much I hate *feelings*?

Just as I'm in the middle of my own self-imposed pity party, who should darken my door? Someone from my past with whom I've had no communication with for a very long time and for a very *good* reason.

The *Rev. John Dowdy*. I grew up listening to his preaching because my parents had the idea that church was the right thing to do. Heck, I always thought it was the right thing to do too. Live your life by God's rules in His world, do right, pray, love Jesus, love your neighbor. All's well with the world, right? *Wrong!* I learned that no amount of doing *right* was in fact *right*. Seeing him just brought up the emotions of five years ago.

"Hello, Jimmy," John said as he smiled compassionately at me.

I *want* to dislike him. I want so badly to just tell him to leave me alone and stay away from me, but I can't. My heart fills with sorrow every time I see him, and I want to cry. *Feelings*—I hate them!

"Hey, preacher" is what I was going for, but you guessed right. "Unnghh, un gung."

"I know you can't talk, son. You've been on my heart so much and for so long," he said in that *way*. He was just so…so…genuine. His crystal-blue eyes displayed so much pain but so much love all at the same time. My soul longed to talk to him and tell him *everything*. I could feel myself fighting back tears. Ahhhhh! More *feelings*!

"Listen, I just came by to tell you that I'm praying for you to get well soon," he said as he leaned over my bed and clasped my hand gently. He slowly turned to walk away. He turned back and looked back at me and came back to the bedside chair, pointing his aged finger in a nonaccusatory wag, and said, "Oh yeah, there was another thing that I wanted to talk to you about," as he sat down on the chair.

Gotta love him. Even though he's in his seventies now, he's spry and sharp as a tack, and I knew in my bones that he'd been saving this up for a long while, probably like five years.

Just as quickly as he sat down, my mind went back many years with thoughts of my father. There was a time that my mother had some issues that required my father to be an absolute saint of a man.

I remember it so clearly. My dad and I were at the breakfast table, and Mom had just finished making breakfast, happy as a lark, or so I thought.

She turned to my dad and yelled, "I never get any of the support that I need from you, and it breaks my heart." She just threw the dish towel on the counter and stormed out of the kitchen.

Bear in mind that I was sitting at the same table with both of them for the past twenty or so minutes, and there wasn't a sideways word said that even amounted to this attack on my father. The breakfast was made, we had eaten, and she was in the process of cleaning up the plates, and my dad was looking at the paper, smoking a cigarette. And after her tirade, he paused and looked over the top of his glasses, and slowly nodded his head and didn't say a word.

"Pop, what's that about? Why didn't you say anything?" I asked in an inquisitive outrage.

"The Lord gave us two ears and one mouth for a reason, son. Your mother's telling me something. Don't rightly know what it is just yet, but I need to *listen*, not just hear," he said as he put the paper down and leaned forward in his chair, pondering my mother's outrage.

My mother had an accident years earlier that jumbled up her head just a bit, and she sometimes had emotional and mental lapses. They got better over time, but they required a *lot* of patience from Dad.

"What does that even mean?" I asked as I got up from the kitchen table, with a typical late-teen attitude. The equivalent of *whatever*.

My dad looked at me and said, "Means that a *man* should be slow to speak, slow to anger, quick to love, quick to forgive, and even quicker to be patient with people because you never know what they're going through," as if he were a swami on a mountaintop.

Just like that, I was transported back to present day with Rev. John Dowdy getting ready to school me in the very same way.

"Naked I came from my mother's womb, and naked I will depart. The Lord gave, and the Lord has taken away. May the name of the Lord be praised. In all this, Job did not sin by charging God with wrong-doing," he said as he looked at me.

"I know, Jimmy. There's not a day that goes by that you don't play that video over and over in your head. I know that your heart is utterly broken, and had I been a better shepherd, I wouldn't have taken your insolence, and you would've heard this years ago, but it wasn't the time. Now is the time, Jimmy. You know that these two events in *your* life have one common denominator. Put on the full armor of God,

Jimmy," he said as if he were giving me marching orders.

What are you even talking about? I thought in my head.

My getting shot in the face has nothing whatsoever to do with my chasing JoJo and killing my parents and crippling my little brother. Maybe Rev wasn't as sharp as I thought. But then in a ponderance that came from nowhere, I questioned myself. I hadn't put the two together. I didn't think about it. Is that even possible? Is it possible that my cloak-and-dagger investigation into the mayor after the accident led up to *this*?

CHAPTER 11

PERSONAL OR PROFESSIONAL?

Rebellion to tyrants is obedience to God.

—Benjamin Franklin
(proposed as the motto for the
Great Seal of the United States)

I hadn't put those pieces together. Was Dowdy right? Once again, after the good reverend left, all there was to do was think.

Eleven months after the accident in 1985

I followed Calvin Jackson because I knew he was dirty. Deep down in my very being, I knew that he and Mayor Albritton, whom I had named *the don of the ghetto*, were up to no good, and I was going to prove it. So I made it my job to let Calvin know that he wasn't untouchable, or at least that was my plan.

After the accident, I had all but cut the world out. The only thing that mattered to me was my wife, my newborn baby girl, my little brother, and my job. Denny was living with us, and it ate my guts to know that Jackson and Albritton were getting away with trafficking cocaine. If I hadn't chased JoJo, I wouldn't have killed my parents and maimed my brother. I was mad, and I was on a single mission—to take the garbage out. The only *feeling* that was allowed in my body was anger.

*****

As I lay in that hospital bed and recounted my attempts to bring down the "don" of the ghetto, what Dowdy said made sense, but why would he even suggest this connection? It's crazy that this even came out of his brain, much less his mouth. Man, this is a stretch. Was this some sort of divine intervention? Then the overarching conspiracy question was, how could Albritton have known that I'd be right there at the right time to take the robbery as bait?

As I thought back, I remembered being held over after a midnight shift to *answer* for my actions during my shift.

*****

"Mack! Major wants you ASAP," Sergeant Dillon announced as I was signing off my last report.

I knocked on the major's partially open door, recognizing the mayor sitting in the office, laughing with the major, who motioned me to come in.

"You know Mayor Albritton," Major Carpenter assumed.

"Can't say that I do. You needed me, sir?" I said rather smugly and with a notable disdain.

"The mayor has a business interest and a young protégé he's helped get off the streets that you may know—Calvin Jackson," Carpenter informed me, as if announcing good deeds and presenting the prince of Egypt.

"I'm familiar with Calvin Jackson, yes, sir,"

"It seems that you've become somewhat overly interested in the young man, and the mayor would like to know what this was about," Carpenter inquired with an indignant and rather arrogant tone.

"I wasn't aware that the mayor needed to know the operation of every aspect of the police department, sir," I retorted.

Carpenter, a rather short-fused man, stood up from his desk and leaned over his desk and was preparing to tear my backside from one coast to the other but was interrupted by Albritton, causing Carpenter to return to his seat.

"I apologize for the way this appears, Mr. Mack," Albritton said as he stood up from the chair with the most hesitantly businesslike demeanor.

"That's officer," I corrected the mayor's incorrect identification. After all, I was on duty, and we were talking about my officer-related persona.

With a begrudged smirk on his face and while buttoning his $1,000 business jacket, Albritton said, "Officer, then. Mack. However, a bright young man such as Mr. Jackson has always fallen on the, let's say, less-than-friendly side of the legal system and deserves a hand up," as if giving a speech to a local society club, much like that of charismatic leaders of the past, all with the bells and whistles of hand gestures and body language designed to intimate emotions.

"So I have chosen to mentor young Calvin by giving him entrepreneurial training and the opportunities that will allow him to claw his way back onto the *right* side of the law," he continued, rather pompously, I might add. His demeanor actually nauseated me. As if he is a generous millionaire who was concerned for "all the people" and making sure that everyone knew to praise him. You know the kind of guy I'm talking about. Fake! Fake, fake, fake!

"How is it that I'm interfering with your philanthropic and entrepreneurial training camp?" I asked in a nonthreatening and nonsarcastic tone. But you know, I don't think that neither he nor the major appreciated my choice of phraseology.

Carpenter launched himself out of his chair and threw a stiffly pointed finger toward me.

"You listen to me! Unless you have a really good reason, you best leave Calvin Jackson alone. Got it? Good! Dismissed."

*****

There was another time, totally by accident. I stopped a car one night for weaving over the yellow line. It was driven by Jackson, and he was drunk as a skunk, so guess what I got when signing off.

"Mack!" Dillon yelled.

"Let me guess," I interrupted.

"Major wants," Dillon and I said in unison.

I performed the ritualistic air knock on Carpenter's door, and he looked up.

"What did I tell you?" Carpenter bellowed like a bull.

"What I recall you saying, sir, is that unless I had *good* reason, I needed to leave Jackson alone. Isn't that what you said?" I replied, and before he could say anything else, I added, "Isn't enforcing traffic laws part of my job, sir?"

"You're cutting it close," Carpenter said as he squinted at me with disgust.

"I didn't know it was him. Otherwise, I'd been more than happy to let him swerve across the yellow line and kill someone. Would that be acceptable for you, sir?" I snapped back with just as much contempt as I could muster.

"Get out!"

Surprisingly enough, young Prince Jackson never stayed more than forty-five minutes in jail and never had to appear in court. Funny, huh?

*****

Then there was a robbery of Southside Corner Market, and unfortunately, I was the reporting offi-cer. Go, Team Jimmy! With Mr. Calvin Jackson being the manager of this fine establishment, he was the caller and reporter.

"Mr. Jackson, is everyone okay?" I asked as I entered the store.

Jackson looked at me with hate and immediately blew out his breath in a deep and heavy sigh, as if to say, "Oh, brother."

"Yeah, no one was hurt. He got like $150," Jackson said.

With a supersurprised look on my face that let everyone know that I was shocked, I said, "Huh, 150 bucks? You keep that in the till?" I asked in total disbelief.

"Yeah. You know I cash folks' checks and all," Jackson replied.

"Mr. Jackson, I know it's your store and all, but that's just not good. I mean bad guys talk and everything. You know, they may get some ideas that you make it easy."

"What are you saying, Mack? You sayin' something?" Jackson said in complete offense and that look that said he wanted to start a fight.

"I'm not *sayin'* anything other than what you're hearing. Listen to me. Bad guys talk. Bad guys plot. Bad guys take the easy way out, and if you're an easy way, you're gonna get robbed again and again. Simple, not rocket science," I said with a tone of aggravation at his senseless offense.

Yep, you guessed it.

"Mack!" Dillon announced, as if it's becoming commonplace, leaning into the bullpen and knocking on the doorframe,

"Major wants to see me," I replied, as if omniscient.

"Right," Dillon confirmed and shook his head as he retreated.

Knock, knock, blah, blah.

"Why are you insulting Calvin Jackson and inferring that he's in concert with the robber? He was the victim of a crime and deserves dignity," Carpenter asked, as if poor Calvin was the one who had the gun stuffed in his face.

I looked at Carpenter as if he just said that two plus two was nine.

"What?" I said in disbelief.

"Calvin Jackson was the reporter. He wasn't the *victim* of anything. It's not even his money. Sally Washington was the *victim*—his employee, I might add. She had a gun stuffed in *her* face demanding the money. And I quote, 'All of it. I know there's more,'" I said as I leaned over Carpenter's desk, reminding him that I was the one who was there.

"You have no proof that Calvin Jackson has anything to do with this."

"And I made *no* inference that he did. I don't really care *how* he took it. He said he keeps $150 in the till, and I reminded him that this isn't a wise choice. He's the one that went down the whole what-you-sayin' rabbit hole. So I'm not the one that needs to be in the hot seat right now, and you need to quit being Albritton's do boy, sir," I replied as I pleaded my case and pointed over Carpenter's desk at him in a very obvious nonfiltered recitation of facts.

Carpenter looked up from the paperwork on his desk and over the frames of his glasses and, uncharacteristically calm, said, "I don't like your tone."

"And I don't like this harassment for doing my job."

"It seems to me that you might need a reminder of who you are and who you are not. I believe that a ten-day suspension is just what you need to remind you and maybe refresh your sensibilities," Carpenter said in a very cold, collected, and almost happy tone. "You need to wait outside while I prepare this letter. Enjoy your unpaid leave, Officer Mack."

*****

There were other instances involving Jackson, but none of them were malicious on my part. I was discreetly watching him and the mayor. Not a big deal. If nothing was going on, I wouldn't find anything, right? Most of these encounters with Jackson were what most folks would call coincidence. Did I mention that I don't believe in coincidence? The more the police department told me to stay away from Jackson, the more I tried, but the shift commanders always put me on that side of town, always on that beat.

Wait a minute, I thought, as if struck by lightning.

If they wanted me to leave Jackson alone, all they had to do was reassign me, right? Put me on day shift, traffic detail, the other side of town and away from the source, right? Why didn't they do that? If the all-powerful Carpenter was so intent on having me leave Calvin Jackson alone, why didn't he make it happen? My actions never amounted to anything more than smarting off to him that time in the office. Nothing that could get me or the department sued, I said to myself with sincerity and conviction.

Could it be that my parents' death could be traced back to Albritton and Jackson after all? And the only thing that made Jackson, Albritton, and now, Carpenter, uneasy was me, the only *possible* link? I hadn't even considered this *link*, especially five years later. How can this be an issue now?

CHAPTER 12

AND SO IT BEGINS

I can't believe this, but I need you, Grundy.

—Jimmy Mack

I've been in this hospital room for ten days, and for once, I'm excited to see a doctor. My bandages are supposed to come off, and they *might* unwire my jaws. This is good.

"Good morning, Jimmy," Dr. Henderson said as he sauntered into my room, going over to the windows to open the blinds.

Seven thirty in the morning, and the guy looks like he's been awake all day. Hair in place, freshly showered, happy, smiling, I thought to myself, and I was not feeling as *fresh* as the good doctor.

Pffft, I blew out my breath.

"Let's have a look, shall we?" he said as he turned on every possible light and began dismantling the mummy wrappings from my face, humming some happy tune.

He must be on drugs. Who's happy at this time of day? I thought.

As the wrapping became less and less and more and more light was being allowed into my eyes, I felt the need to squint my eyes to dampen the brightness that was flooding my eyes.

In the doorway I could see that Mary had just arrived, leaning against the doorframe, and her hand was kind of *smooshing* her lips as she awaited the results.

Dr. Henderson finished the demummification and sat back and said, "Huh," with a somewhat puzzled look on his face.

This guy is really odd, I thought to myself, picking up on the fact that he obviously had a breath mint so as to not make me smell morning breath.

"That looks really good, Jimmy," he said as he placed his face close to mine, examining my entire face and left ear. "Can you hear anything in this ear?" he asked.

It sounds like you're talking in a garbage can, I answered to myself.

He turned to look at Mary and said, "Come on over. I'd like you meet your husband." He smiled.

With tears in her eyes, she slowly came to the bed and kept her hand over her mouth.

"Oh, my sweet baby," she said as she began lightly sobbing, and she hugged me.

"Ung, ung, ungg, unggg," was all I could come up with, which meant, "How do I look?"

"Would you like me to wait on the jaws?" Dr. Henderson asked in a very pleasant manner.

Mary quickly moved out of the way to allow Dr. Henderson into the correct position to continue his examination. He began moving my lips, feeling my lower jaw, and massaging my jaws at the hinge points, all while looking up and humming. Then I recognized the tune he was humming: "What a friend we have in Jesus." I got a chill, and tears began filling my eyes.

He leaned back and patted me on my left thigh.

"I think we've got a winner. I'm going to schedule a time this afternoon to get those wires out. It's not like pulling out stitches, you know, so I need you to be a little more patient with me. We'll give you a little sedative, take out the hardware, and get you fitted for a prosthesis, and go from there. It's a good day. Good day indeed," he said without ever losing his boyish smile, and he turned to exit the room, humming.

Mary was staring at me as if she hadn't seen me in a million years, cupping my face in her hands and examining me with her eyes in bewilderment.

"Jimmy, this is a miracle. I thought half of your face was gone but it's not. It's not that bad at all," she said, hugging me and then pushing back and hugging me again.

She quickly jumped up from the side of the bed and ran out of the room. "I'm going to get a mirror."

I wonder what would've happened if it didn't *look good*, I thought kind of sarcastically to myself as the morphine maintained my grumpy demeanor.

She returned to the room and presented the mirror, as if an offering to the king. As I took the mirror, I couldn't help but hesitate a little, and I held it face down on my chest. I looked up to the ceiling and brought the mirror to my line of sight.

What looks so good about this? I thought.

I've got the Grand Canyon running down the left side of my face, and half my left ear is gone. What are they seeing that's so "great"? I dropped the mirror to my chest, and Mary looked at me with a puzzled look.

"What's wrong, sweetie," she asked as if she really didn't know.

I closed my eyes and took a deep breath. I wanted to unsee what I saw. I mean, sure, I wasn't a really great lookin' guy to start with, but really? This scar literally zigzagged from just under my left cheek just about at the corner of my mouth and went all the way down my face and terminated in my ear. The stitches reminded me of the Frankenstein character, pieces of stuff just sewn together with stitches fit for a cadaver. Sure, the ear was sewn back together, but that little doohickey that is supposed to jut out from my ear was gone. And it just looked funny to me. I had to get a grip.

Wait, Jimmy. What did you just ask yourself? What if it didn't turn out well? What would Mary do? You've got your answer, don't you, you ungrateful man? It didn't turn out well, but she's here, and she thinks it's great, I thought as I chastised myself, and Mary obviously saw me arguing with myself, but I decided to be grateful and rubbed Mary's arm and smiled with my eyes.

They say that you look in someone's eyes to see if they're smiling. Apparently, that's true because I couldn't feel my mouth smiling, but I was smiling inside when I saw how happy Mary was, and she smiled back at me. It made me *feel* great, and I forgot that whole conversation with myself and the complaint about my appearance. Wow! I never thought I'd *like* a *feeling*. It had been so long since I felt any feelings other than anger.

An orderly wheeled into the room and announced, "Must be your lucky day, pal. Doc got you in."

As he wheeled me to what I thought was an operating room, I could only think about everything that transpired over the past ten days. I'm alive, but I shouldn't be. I look like death eating a biscuit, but no one else sees it or at least admits it. The preacher led me to an epiphany. But where was Denny? Much to my chagrin, I have *feelings* that I need to deal with.

"Okay, Jimmy, a little knockout here, and we'll be on our way," Dr. Henderson said as the nurse and anesthesiologist were preparing.

As I woke up, I could only feel pain. It was like I brushed my teeth with a wire toothbrush. But I realized that my lips were apart, but man, did it hurt to move my jaw even a little.

"It's going to take a little bit," a young nurse who was checking my vitals said.

"A little bit for what?" I mumbled.

"You know—soreness, movement, learning how to move your jaw again."

I unknowingly clinched my jaw, and I screamed in pain, causing the nurse to look at me and say, in a matter-of-fact, no-nonsense kind of way, "Now, I reckon you shouldn't do that again for now, hmm."

All I could do was laugh because her delivery of that line was great. She never cracked a smile or let on that what she said was really kind of funny.

I guess I dozed off because I woke up in my room with Mary sitting there and Covey standing by her.

"Hey, big guy," Covey smiled as he rubbed my arm.

"What's goin' on with your bad self?" I mumbled, and Covey's eyes immediately got really big, and he had this excited expression on his face, like showing your puppy his favorite toy.

"I can understand you, dude," he said, fully animated and with his best shocked face.

"Ha…ha…ha. You are *so* funny, Covey," I said in my drab, sarcastic tone.

"Hey, Mary, baby, can you go get me a cup of ice please," I mumbled to Mary. Mary leaned over and kissed me on the forehead and held my hand a second longer, smiled, and walked out. She knew me. She knew I needed to talk to Covey. Even though I didn't ask her to leave, she just somehow knew.

I could tell because of the little smile that said, "I understand." She knew I'd always protect her from the badge.

"Covey, come here, man," I mumbled to Covey, motioning with my hand for him to come closer.

"I need help here. This wasn't a robbery gone south," I said with a partially closed mouth and in agonizing pain.

Covey pulled back from me like he'd seen a ghost.

"What are you saying, Jimmy? You sayin' that IA was right?" He backed up like he was dirty for even being close to me.

"No, no, nothing like an IA special. Wait. IA? Right? About what?" I began to get nervous as I realized that IA had grilled Covey about me.

"Grundy. Grundy hinted that the robbery was *your* setup, that…that you *knew* the suspect and took him out over something you're into," he said as he got more and more nervous and started to pace back and forth.

"Wait a minute now!" I yelled, and I regretted it because the pain was horrendous.

"I just figured this out three days ago. Why did Grundy think this way *my* action?" I asked in an escalating and nervous tone, rubbing my left jaw and moving it side to side manually with my hand.

"What'd you do, Jimmy?" Covey asked, pleading for answers.

"I didn't *do* anything, Covey. I'm the victim here," I began to explain.

"I've been secretly watching Jackson and Albritton for the past four years, but I guess they found out and wanted me out of the picture," I explained.

"What do you mean, *watching*? Investigating the mayor and his protégé? You nuts?" Covey was getting more and more upset as he continued to pace.

"Who's this…this Grundy?" I asked in a miffed tone.

"He's the IA stiff running lead on your shoot," he answered with a headshake of disbelief, putting his hand to his forehead.

"I need to talk to him, Covey."

CHAPTER 13

CORRUPTION ABOUNDS

It's hard, when you're up to your
armpits in alligators, to remember you
came here to drain the swamp.

—Ronald Reagan

I was actually kind of nervous. Covey reached out to Grundy like I'd asked, and he was heading up today. How do I prove this? I mean, what *real* evidence do I have against the duo of Albritton and Jackson. Sure, I've got a lot of circumstantial stuff, but what do I *really* have? And to accuse the mayor of setting me up for a hit? Maybe Covey's right. I am nuts.

Grundy walked into my hospital room holding a rather large accordion file folder, and it seemed like he had a bit of an attitude. But that was *my* first impression. You could look at him and tell that he was cop, probably an uptight kind of guy but unassuming and no-nonsense. But you could definitely tell that his butt was right up there on his shoulders.

"Mack," Grundy said as he entered the room, rolling his tongue across the front of his teeth as if he was irritated beyond belief to be there.

"Yeah. You Grundy? Got ID?" I snapped back, matching his attitude.

He flipped open his ID case, which I snatched from his hand, and I examined him with my eyes, glancing between the photo and the man. I tossed it back to him.

"Anybody know that you're here?" I asked.

"What are you, deep throat? I guess you're gonna ask if I was followed too, right?" Grundy snapped back with an agitated sarcasm.

"Sorry," I said as I exhaled and leaned back on the bed, readjusting my jaw.

"You know, this is all a little *convenient* if you ask me," he said, matching his disbelief with his body language as he stood next to the bed looking down on me, figuratively and physically.

"You wanting to talk to me after your buddy Covington doesn't like my questions about your shoot and…and, getting all Sherlock Holmes and guessing that I think you're dirty," Grundy continued as he adjusted his belt and neck, like he had some sort of *tic* or something when he got worked up.

I just looked at him with a puzzled look on my face and asked in disbelief, "Why would you think I'm dirty? I've bled blue for the better part of ten years, commended three times. Dirty? Covey never told me this."

Grundy had a look on his face as he realized that he'd just revealed the fact that he'd been looking at me for criminal activity and quickly tried to recover with a stuttering question. "What'd you want with me, Mack? I've gotta lot going on and don't have a lot of patience for wasted time."

I shook my head in disbelief that IA had an open jacket on me. This completely deflated me. After all, I'd worked so hard to be one of the *good* guys.

"Albritton's dirty," I said with relief in my voice.

"Wait. You're rattin' out the mayor? You're one of the biggest coke dealers in this town, and you're rattin' out the mayor? You drive keys of coke up from Florida, and you're rattin' out the mayor?" Grundy rattled off an entire court-worthy closing argument.

"That's rich. I gotta hand it to you. I can't find where you're stashing the money, but I did *not* see this coming," he said with a head bounce all while biting his bottom lip and adjusting his neck. Grundy was a very odd and animated character, and he's pretty tightly wound.

"What are *you* smokin'?" I asked Grundy as I looked at him with my head tilted to one side, as if I'd just seen a three-headed cat.

"October 4 through 7, two years ago, you took three days off, drove to Miami in a rental car, changed it for another car at Miami Central Parking, and drove back. The contents of the change car was five kilos of uncut cocaine. That's what I'm talking about," Grundy testified.

"I took three days off to take my daughter to Disney in *Orlando*. No rental car, no exchange— none of that is right. So check your facts before you start throwing that around, Detective," I began raising my voice and getting really angry, and I almost came out of the bed.

Grundy squinted his eyes just a bit and looked at me and said, "Disney?" he said in disbelief.

"Yeah, Disney," I said smugly.

"Then why do I have a picture of you behind the wheel of New Yorker coming out of a parking garage in Miami?" He inquired in a very low, controlled tone without moving any of body or head.

"I've never even been to Miami," I said, "and I certainly have never rented a Chrysler New Yorker. I don't know what photo you have of me, but it ain't right."

Grundy tossed a black-and-white photo on my chest and said, "Explain this, Officer Mack."

There it is, a photo of *me* behind the wheel of, yes, a Chrysler New Yorker. What was *I* smokin'? I felt like I was in a really bad sci-fi movie with my body having been taken over by some mind-controlling alien. But as I looked at the picture, something didn't look quite right to me. Something wasn't right with the shadows. In the photo, the light on my face was coming from my left side, but on the dashboard in the car, the light was not as bright and was coming from the right. It wasn't an in-your-face, supernoticeable difference, but I know that I've never driven a New Yorker in my life, and I know that I've never been to Miami.

"Did you notice this?" I asked Grundy as I extended the photo back toward him and pointing at my face in the photo.

"Notice what?" he asked in a huffy tone.

"The light. It's coming from two directions." I pointed out in an instructional manner.

"What? What do you mean?"

"The light, Dick Tracy!" I said as I tapped the photo. "On my face, it's on the left. On the dashboard, it's on the right. Light doesn't do that. This has been monkeyed with."

Monkeyed with—that's a technical police term used when the speaker has had too many painkillers, by the way.

He snatched the photo from my hand and collapsed into the chair and stared off into another universe with disbelief. I think it could be disbelief that he hadn't noticed that or maybe that he was being used.

The huge accordion file folder labeled "Mack: 88-IAB-291C" fell from his lap as he realized that he'd been a stooge, his mouth agape with his pasty round face losing all color. Not that he had much color to start with.

I felt bad for him. I recognized that look. He was doing the *right* thing, or so he thought. And putting me away was the right thing based on what he knew. It was that moment that you see on those *National Geographic* TV shows where the lioness catches a young impala, which desperately fights by butting his head against the lioness in hopes of regaining freedom, and in an instant, compassion strikes the heart of the lioness, and instead of devouring the young impala, she begins mothering it. I was that young impala, and Grundy was the lioness. Well, figuratively, but you get my drift. He looked at me and said, "I am *so* sorry. Everything I've gotten, the photo and the CI, has shown you as the cop that got tired of doing the right thing and went south. It never even dawned on me that *you* were the target of Carpenter all along," he said in a state of total disbelief.

Mary walked through the door and saw Grundy, whom she'd never met, in this pile of defeat in the chair, and she looked at me.

"Should I come back?" she asked with a hesitantly soft voice as she was putting her purse on the cabinet behind the chair Grundy was sitting in.

Her voice launched Grundy back into reality, and he stood up to yield the chair to her but rushed to gather the scattered contents of the file folder from the floor in an effort to keep her from seeing any of it.

"Uh, no, no, ma'am. I'm just wrapping up here. I'll be leaving now," Grundy announced, which completely took me off guard.

"Leave?" I asked in disbelief.

"Yes, leave, Officer Mack. I will, uh, I will come back tomorrow after I've checked…checked out this new evidence," he stuttered with a frustrated look on his face.

"What do you mean that I was the target of Carpenter?" I demanded as I started to get worked up. "What does he have to do with this?"

Grundy looked around and was obviously very uncomfortable. Now I was really fueled and started to get up out of the bed. Grundy motioned for me to calm down and stay down. He ran his hand over his face.

"He's the one that gave me the photo, said he got it from a source," Grundy explained.

I could only lean back and look at him in disbelief. Why would Carpenter do this to me?

"You're right, Grundy. You need to go," I said rather softly.

Mary had a very confused look on her face as she watched Grundy leave.

"What was *that* about?" Mary asked inquisitively.

"It's a little complicated, sweetie, but I'll have to explain later. I'm glad you're here."

CHAPTER 14

THE PIECES FALL
IN PLACE

Let no one lose heart on account of this
Philistine; your servant will go and fight him.

—David to King Saul

Grundy hadn't come back as promised. It'd been a
week, and I was being discharged today. I was going
home but hadn't heard anything else from Grundy.

Tangled Christmas lights again. A tangled web
of emotions and feelings—the things I was trying to
get used to again. I hadn't seen my baby girl in three
weeks, and I wasn't sure that she was going to accept
me. I know my daughter is *gifted* in many ways, but
that may not translate to accepting the disfigurement
on her father's face.

"Daddy!" Hannah squealed with glee as she ran through the doorway with outstretched arms, attacking me as I was sitting on the chair, waiting for Mary to bring me some clothes to go home in.

"There's my baby girl," I said as I felt my heart melt as my little girl hugged me as tight as an anaconda.

Man, that's what I needed. A hug from my little princess melted my heart every time, and it *felt* great. I'd come to terms with *feelings* while I was in here. Well, I'm a work in progress, and I've learned a lot. I heard a lot, but what I learned most is that sometimes, shutting my big ole mouth lets me *hear* from someone else. Someone with whom I've been at odds with for five years.

I've been stuck between the badge and a hard place for a long time. I fought a really good fight against the evil of mankind without realizing that I was losing my fight for my soul. I blamed God for taking my parents and my being the instrument for that loss, but what I realized was that God doesn't waste opportunities. Just because something happens doesn't mean God was the author of that scene. Without my knowing it, He guided my brother to His calling, fueled a fire in me to fight a giant, and that He was going to bring down that giant in this town and use me in the process, a giant that was beating his chest in pride and arrogance, a metaphorical "Goliath."

"It's not *that* bad," Hannah smiled as she scrutinized and touched the healing scar that slalomed across my left cheek, looking like railroad tracks.

She was so "adult," so smart, so kind, so loving, and so very, well, honest. But it wasn't malicious in a snobby way; it was just facts. I think most kids are brutally honest because it's natural, so my baby girl might not be supernatural, but to me, she was.

Mary came in with a smile and a duffel bag. Her face glowed with joy as she saw me united with my little girl. It was similar to the glow of a pregnant woman. Mary sat her purse and duffel down and stayed back a bit to let me and Hannah have a minute.

"The last time I saw you, you looked like a mummy," Hannah said sheepishly.

"When were you here, baby?" I looked between her and Mary, and Mary's face lost a little color as she was not prepared for *that* revelation.

"After I talked to God," Hannah said with a no-nonsense, by-the-way manner of speaking.

I know that the look on my face was probably indescribable and filled with curiosity because I felt my eyebrows slam together and my eyes squint. I tilted my head a bit and looked at Mary and started to ask, but Mary moved off of the cabinet that she was leaning on and came toward me and Hannah.

"I didn't tell you, Jimmy, because you have enough going on. But after you first got here, Hannah saw me crying in the bedroom and asked me what was wrong," she continued with a thoughtful expression on her face, and she sat down on the bed next to the chair with a confessional relief and big exhale. "Long story short, she knew I lied about where you were and called me out on it. She told me that God told her you were okay, and the next thing I knew, she was putting on her jacket and *telling* me that she was coming to see you." Mary kind of shrugged her shoulders and let out a big breath, as if relieved to have the story told.

"And you were asleep when I brought her here. But she insisted, and honestly, she's been a rock for me through all this," Mary said with a disbelieving sigh and a gentle nod.

I had no words. I could only hold Hannah's little arms in my hands and hold her at arm's length a bit to examine her with my eyes, and with her huge crystal-blue eyes looking into mine, she said the most profound thing that anyone could've ever said to me, especially considering that I had not been the religious leader of our house that I should've been: "God's got this, Daddy."

Immediately, my mind went through every single thought that I had since being here. Reverend Dowdy reminding me of the common denominator; the doctor humming, "What a friend we have in Jesus"; the revelation of the doctored evidence in internal affairs; the surveillance notes that I have against Albritton and Jackson; the knowledge that Carpenter was part of this; the fact that no one thought that my disfigured face was *that bad*—it all sort of melded together to form this sense of cohesiveness and this feeling of triumphant destiny…all in the matter of a split second.

"God's got…got what, baby?" I asked gently and hesitantly as I looked at her and then Mary. Apparently, my little girl has a *very close* relationship to God, which shocked, amazed, and befuddled me beyond words because it certainly wasn't because of anything that I'd done.

By this time, my little girl was "my little girl" again. Being that kid who felt uncomfortable when being asked about something they had just said, she was fiddling with the front of my hospital gown and not looking at me in the eye anymore. She just shrugged her little shoulders and kept to the task of fiddling with the collar of my hospital gown.

I cupped the back of her head and gently brought it to my chest as I looked at Mary and mouthed, "What is this?" We sat there for a few minutes. I, enjoying my family, holding my little girl with her beautiful mother there by my side—Hannah's right. *He does* "got this."

I gently put Hannah to the floor and said, "Okay, baby, Daddy's got to get dressed so we can go home."

"Okay," she said aloofly and just turned to walk out of the room. Mary and I just looked at each other and gave a mutual shoulder shrug with matching facial expressions that say, "Okay then," as Mary walked out and closed the door.

As I put on my clothes, I thought about the battle that I had in front of me. All of the circumstantial stuff was just that—circumstantial. But could I corroborate it? And could I corroborate it *without* Grundy and that photo? This is gonna be such a nightmare, I thought. I really *am* stuck in this job. I can't *not* be a cop anymore. It's all I know. I guess we can move. Yeah, but still a cop with the cop mentality. Humph!

As I tied my shoes, a knock came at the door.

"Just a sec," I said, and as I got up from the chair, the blood rushed from my head, and I got really dizzy and lost my balance. It took me a few seconds to regain my balance, but I opened the door, and there was Hannah with a huge smile of achievement, holding Detective Grundy's hand.

CHAPTER 15

THE BATTLE BELONGS TO THE LORD

I don't know if you know just how tough this is gonna be, but getting shot in the face might end up seeming like a walk in the park.

—Det. Dean Grundy

I woke up at *my* house, in *my* bed, and it was great. I never knew how much I'd taken for granted, but it was all becoming so very crystal clear. I'd *wasted*—yes, *wasted*—the last five years of my life thinking that I was a good guy because of my job and never *appreciating* everything that was there in front of me. The things that didn't cost money, things that were actually *blessings*: my wife, my daughter, my brother…

Oh, my Lord. Denny, I thought as I held my face in my hand, and my heart sank deep into my soul.

"Hey, sweetie," Mary sang as she came into the room, now filled with the great aroma of the cup of coffee in her hand. She flounced onto the side of the bed, leaning down and giving me something I'd missed so much—a soft good-morning kiss.

"Are you feeling okay?" she inquired. She must've deduced from my hand covering my face that I was hurting.

"Yeah, yeah, I'm fine, baby. Have you seen Denny?" I asked with a deep exhale.

She looked at me in astonishment, and her mouth fell agape, and she nodded.

"Yeah. He snuck into the hospital every day to check on you but asked that if anyone saw him, they'd not say. Why?" she asked with a curious look on her face.

"I gotta make it right, sweetie. This whole"—I tried to intimate with hand gestures and facial expressions—"garbage. I gotta make it right with him."

Mary's eyes filled with tears as she fell on me to hug me, kissing my cheeks and then my mouth.

"That's probably one of the nicest, most mature things I've heard you say, Jimmy Mack," she said with a joy-filled voice.

"I'll give him a call right now," she said as she ran out of the room to call Denny. I don't know why she didn't just use the extension in the bedroom, except to think that she didn't want me to hear the rejection of my little brother.

I lay there staring at the ceiling with a pounding headache. It felt like my eyes were being punched by Santa's elves from the inside, and the left side of my head felt like a blowtorch was burning my skull, but I didn't want the oxy.

"Dear Lord, my head hurts so bad," I whispered. "I have not said thank You, but thank You. Please, please forgive me, Lord. I've wasted so much time, and I never recognized that Your plans trump my plans."

Mary bounced back into the room with the announcement that Denny was on his way over, which totally surprised me because I thought for sure that he wouldn't want to see the conscious me. Let me explain.

Being seven years older than Denny and being responsible for our parent's death *and* the loss of his right leg weighed really heavy on me. Even though he stayed with me and Mary after he got out of the hospital, we drifted really far apart, and I never talked to him about the accident. I never let him know how

I *felt*. I never asked him how he *felt*. I never told him that if Mary hadn't been pregnant with Hannah, I wanted to commit suicide. I never told him that I was so happy that he survived and that I was proud of everything he'd accomplished despite his losses. I never cried with him to grieve our individual and collective loss. I never laughed with him after the accident. I never took time to be his older brother after the accident. The accident not only killed our parents, but it also killed our relationship, which was *my* fault. With the grudge that I had against God after the accident, I couldn't stomach the fact that he wanted to go into the ministry. It made me mad at him. I knew that God was in charge, but to me, it seemed like He was being mean to us, punishing me, punishing Denny. So I chose to distance myself from Denny and God.

I'd gotten dressed and was sitting at the kitchen table with my left ear toward the small alcove leading to the entry door, so I hadn't heard him knock. I didn't know it, but Mary and Denny were standing at the doorway, looking at me while I stared out into the backyard, taking in the greenery and...life. All of a sudden, I felt a light touch on my shoulder and looked over to see Denny smiling at me. I felt the same melting of my heart that I have when I see

Hannah or Mary, and I stood up and wrapped my arms around him and fell sobbing onto his shoulder. He must've thought I was crazy as he just patted the back of my head, whispering, "It's okay, Jimmy. God's got this."

All of a sudden, the tears stopped, and I pushed back from his embrace and asked in astonishment, "What did you just say?"

"I said, God's got this," he said with an angelic smile that I'd never noticed him have before. Not that I'd noticed anything about my brother over the past five years, but he had the same quality that Reverend Dowdy has, and I just now saw it. It was amazing. My little brother, my daughter, Reverend Dowdy—they all have a tight relationship with *Him*, and they're in *my* life trying to help *me*. That means that *He really does* "got this."

Out of nowhere, five years not even considering the *Word*, my mind went right to the Bible. "What shall we then say to these things? If God be for us, who can be against us?"

I looked at my baby brother and examined him with my eyes while I held him back at arm's length,

"I-I have been so, so very wrong, Den. I'm sorry," I said with my voice quivering, but he interrupted me. "Wrong about what, Jimmy? Hurt people *hurt* people. I should apologize to *you*. I let you suffer in pain in your own prison even though *I* knew better. *I* should've come to you to help you through it. I can't imagine the burden of guilt that you must've put on yourself, but I didn't know *how* to approach you," he said sympathetically, and eyes filled with compassion.

"You wouldn't have been able to talk to me, Denny. I shut everyone, except Mary and Hannah out, and sometimes even them. I buried myself in seeking revenge that I lost sight of anything that is truly important. I'm sorry," I said as I hugged him again, both of us with healing tears dribbling down our cheeks.

Don't get me wrong. I still don't like *feelings*, but I felt relief in so many ways. So many burdens have left me, and I *felt* lighter. I could actually breathe a little easier, but I still have to talk to John Dowdy because I was such a jerk to him.

I looked at Mary and then Denny and said, "Mary. Denny, I have to apologize and ask that you forgive me for being…"

Both of them looked to the floor shaking their head uncomfortably as if not wanting to address the elephant in the room.

"A jerk," I continued.

"So much has happened over the past three weeks," I explained, causing them both to look at each other with puzzled expressions.

"I have so much to tell you, guys, but I have to make a call right now," I said as I backed out of the kitchen and headed to the bedroom.

Mary looked at Denny and asked, "He's been in a hospital bed for three weeks with his mouth wired shut. What could have happened?" with a curious expression.

I dialed Grundy's number with a sense of urgency, and he picked up, "Grundy," he snapped into the phone.

"Grundy, this is Mack. Can you meet me at my house?" I asked while anticipating a yes.

I could hear that Grundy had slammed a door. I could only assume it was his office door because he didn't want anyone to hear our conversation.

"I can, but not right now," he almost whispered into the phone.

"I gotta figure out if Dirkson's in the mix," he said, exhaling strongly.

"Yeah, yeah, I get it," I said in frustration.

"I just…I just have to do this, Grundy. It feels important and so, so urgent. You know what I mean?" I asked frantically.

Grundy began talking to someone who'd obviously come into his office, and I could only get pieces of it, but it had to be Dirkson.

"I'm on my way, Jimmy. Gimme fifteen," Grundy said and then a dial tone.

As I hung up the phone, my heart was beating in my already-pounding head, my mouth was dry, and I was feeling like I was going to pass out or vomit or both. I tried to quickly regain my composure as I went back into the kitchen, putting on a *fake* smile.

CHAPTER 16

HERE WE GO!

Veni, vidi, vici.

—Julius Caesar

A brash knock came at my front door as I, Mary, and Denny were talking in the kitchen, and the intensity of the knock startled us all. I jumped to my feet to go find out if it was Grundy, and as I opened the door, it wasn't just Grundy, but another person was beside him.

"Jimmy, this is Unit Chief Dirkson," Grundy presented Dirkson with a submissive lowered head.

I know that I must've had to look like I just saw my own death coming because I felt my face lose all blood flow, and my mouth fell agape. Both men quickly rushed past me into *my* house, as if on a mission, and Dirkson spun around and confronted me.

"I'm not gonna play with you, Mack," Dirkson said while getting in my face.

"This is pretty serious, son," he continued with a single eye squint and lowered voice, as if he felt better now that he'd lain down the rules.

I led the two men into the living room, but no one sat down. Dirkson circled around and pointed at Grundy, as if giving a summary. "He's been on your tail for two years now, under the impression that *you're* dirty and bringing coke from Miami…," he continued in an escalating tone.

Mary and Denny had huddled into the doorway, both listening intently.

"And now"—he had an exasperated tone and was still slowly pacing—"now there's proof that Carpenter set you up. Is that right, Officer Mack? Is that…is *that* what you're saying?" he asked in a disbelieving manner, and it was very apparent that he was quite worked up.

Mary and Denny both exchanged disbelieving expressions, not really knowing that what they're hearing is real.

"Chief," Grundy injected, "it's like I told you in the car. The…the proof is this photo that I've got."

Dirkson blew out his breath. "This photo, this photo—what about *this* photo makes any of this garbage real, Dean, huh?" Dirkson blurted with disbelief and disgust on his face as he looked at me as if I was a Sicilian mob boss.

"You remember I took leave last week?" Grundy explained, with Dirkson nodding his head in remembrance.

"Yeah, yeah, so?" Dirkson replied.

"Well…well, I went to the state lab and pulled a favor from a friend of mine. The photo *is* doctored. It's fake. Jimmy wasn't driving the New Yorker."

Dirkson stopped midpace and looked at Grundy. "New Yorker?" Dirkson asked, as if blindsided.

"Yeah, yeah, remember, Carpenter gave me a photo of Jimmy driving a New Yorker exiting a parking garage in Miami in October two years ago with five kilos of coke in the trunk, remember? The convicted doper gave me the goods on Mack, remember?" Grundy was rehashing earlier talks.

"Then why isn't *he* in jail already?" Dirkson fired back, pointing at me and raising his voice.

"The photo needed authenticity from the photographer, who disappeared, and the CI didn't have credibility. So Carpenter never produced the photographer but instead gave me the CI, a CI that couldn't be vetted," Grundy continued.

"Wait a second!" Mary yelled and barged into the living room.

"Two years ago, we took Hannah to Disney, not Miami. Where are you getting this?" Mary demanded, and she was getting pretty upset, I might add.

"Jimmy, what's going on?" she begged as Denny pulled her back toward the kitchen.

"That's the thing, Chief," Grundy said with full conviction in his voice.

"Carpenter *never* gave up the photographer. He also never said *how* the photographer came to be where he was, when he was, in order see what he saw and conveniently photograph it," Grundy finished with conviction.

Dirkson blew out his breath in disbelief as he ran his hand across the top of his balding head and turned away from Grundy.

Dirkson now tried to digest what Grundy just said.

"So the major of the uniform division came to you and said what exactly? I mean…how did he come to *you* and not me? I'm the chief of my unit!" Dirkson yelled in more of an accusatory manner as he just realized that Carpenter had gone around him to get to Grundy.

You know how inconvenient things happen at the wrong time? In walked Hannah, who was just waking up.

"What's going on, Daddy?" Hannah asked in a sleepy little girl voice, and every adult in the house stopped everything. Grundy and Dirkson looked away from Hannah, and Mary rushed in and swooped up Hannah into her arms to take her back to the other end of the house with Denny following close behind.

"Do you have an official report from the lab?" Dirkson asked as he blew out his breath, obviously attempting to calm down and keep his voice down. In suppressed anger, he grabbed his mouth and wiped down into a chin stroke. Dirkson was really keeping it together, and I had to applaud him for it because it looked like the vein in his forehead was going to pop.

"Yes, sir. Yes, I do," Grundy announced as he adjusted his neck.

"I need to use your phone, Jimmy," Dirkson said. I can't really adequately describe the look on his face, except to say that it looked like he was nauseous and needed a bathroom more than a phone.

"Yeah, yeah, sure, go ahead. It's on the wall by the back door." I pointed into the kitchen.

"Chief," I said, interrupting his gait, and he turned back to look at me. I looked at him and Grundy.

"You guys want some coffee or something?" I asked, trying to be hospitable, but neither man seemed to be wanting of the hospitality.

Mary was now at the hall doorway again after putting Hannah back down and leaving Denny with the little one. She watched Dirkson walk through to the kitchen and looked at me and said, "Complicated? Jimmy, this is *not* complicated." She slowly walked forward into the living room, squaring off with me and Grundy watching on, all the while, she had her arms folded.

"This…this…this is undeniably the most absurd thing that I've ever heard. Your boss faked a photo to give to IA to get them to think that you are corrupt?" She looked back and forth between me and Grundy in total confusion, disbelief, and anger.

"It's insane! Jimmy, tell me this is *not* true." She released her folded arms and dropped them to her side and begged, not knowing if she should be mad or scared or both.

"That's not all, Mary." I looked into her eyes as I grabbed her two hands and held them tightly, and I glanced over to Grundy and nodded. He adjusted his neck and started his explanation.

"The man that shot Jimmy, that…that Jimmy killed three weeks ago, was Calvin Jackson's cousin," Grundy explained, causing my head to spin in his direction with such force that I tweaked my neck, and I winced in pain. But Mary didn't know what that meant because she didn't know Calvin Jackson or what that meant.

"When were you gonna tell me that, Grundy?" I demanded as I released Mary's arms and redirected my gaze on Grundy. Mary looked on with total confusion as I lashed out at Grundy with total confusion on her face.

"I-I just found out, Jimmy. I haven't even told Dirkson yet. All this is coming together really, really fast." Grundy bit his bottom lip nervously. "And, well, I've never been involved in anything like this. A major of a police department, the mayor, his crony—all in a conspiracy to take out a beat cop?" he said in disbelief. "C'mon, Jimmy, a beat cop? Really? Not tryin' to speak outta turn here, but in the political world, you're…you're a nobody."

He's right. It makes absolutely no sense what-soever. How could I ever be a threat to any of these guys? I work the midnight shift on the south side. I haven't been promoted and, with my mouth, will *never* be promoted. I come in and do my shift and go home. There is nothing special about me—*nothing*.

Then it hit me right between the eyes, and my body tensed, and I looked at Mary and back at Grundy. An epiphany.

"It was the coke," I said in a soft voice.

Grundy and Mary looked at each other, totally befuddled.

"The coke in JoJo's trunk five years ago. It can be tied to Albritton and Jackson. That's why I needed to be outta the way," I explained. Grundy and Mary were now completely lost.

"Don't you get it? Their fingerprints have to be on the kilos in the trunk and…and probably on the paper bag of cash," I continued.

"That doesn't make sense, Jimmy. Carpenter could've ordered that coke destroyed anytime he wanted after it was tested. You know we don't keep evidence like that," Grundy rationalized. "You're grasping at straws, Jimmy."

"Listen, just listen. Not in this case. I could put JoJo with Jackson, which puts Jackson with Albritton, which puts Albritton with Carpenter. Remember, Albritton was at Southside the night of the chase five years ago. He was inside the market. That's demonstrative evidence of his knowledge of the criminal activity because he and his protégé were there at five in the morning for an early-morning drop of five grand. Only questions are, where was JoJo takin' the coke, and what was the five grand for?" I continued, convinced of my deduction's credibility.

"That doesn't link Carpenter to Albritton until he started hassling you. But his hassling you only looks like a political kiss up. Not a lot to hang your hat on. But they got nervous for some reason about that evidence still being around," Grundy said as he became enlightened but looking for the missing piece.

Denny had been standing at the hallway door leading to the bedrooms, listening, and then he injected. "What are you talking about? None of this makes sense," Denny inserted in a demanding tone and wanting answers, with Mary nodding her head in agreement.

"The robbery was a setup to kill Jimmy. The major and the mayor wanted your husband dead because of the cocaine found in JoJo's car the night of his parent's accident. Plus the added bonus of having

Jimmy labeled a coke dealer, no one will look any further because they'll be able to blame the accident on Jimmy as part of a dope war, and this will take the light off of Jackson and, by proxy, Albritton," Grundy explained.

"That's pretty thin," Dirkson said as he came back into the center of the living room.

"I sure hope that the evidence from JoJo's chase is still around because you're not gonna make this fly without it," Dirkson finished as he plunged his hands deep into his pockets and looked around the room at everyone.

"We've gotta go now. Jimmy, Dean, let's go," Dirkson said.

"We're not done," Mary injected.

"Yeah, we are, at least for now," Dirkson said as he withdrew his hands from his pockets and hoisted his trousers.

"There's a lot left to do, and apparently, we don't have the luxury of time," Dirkson said as he motioned for me and Grundy to leave.

"We've got a meeting with the feds downtown. They want to get this on the books now. Seems that Albritton, Jackson, and Carpenter have already been on the radar for quite some time, and you might have the pieces they need to finish the puzzle. But we need this on the record *today* and ready for grand jury second Tuesday of next month," Dirkson said with an eyebrow raised.

"This is what has them spooked now after five years," I said as I was able to put all the pieces together now. Grundy nodded in agreement.

"Hope you're not busy for the next couple of months," he added as he patted me on the shoulder as we all walked out of the house.

ABOUT THE AUTHOR

Barry McKinley is a Southern Christian fiction author. After spending the better half of forty years in law enforcement, playing music in worship bands, and occasionally preaching the gospel, he's combined his life's witness and work into this and upcoming books. Designed to thrill readers and stimulate faith, his use of colloquial language in his books captivate, engage, and encourage readers to ultimately find individual revelation.